Official
Cambridge
Exam
Preparation

Kid's Box

New Generation

T0384691

British English

Caroline Nixon &
Michael Tomlinson

CAMBRIDGE

Activity Book
with Digital Pack

6

Thanks and Acknowledgements

Authors' thanks

Many thanks to everyone at Cambridge University Press and Assessment for their dedication and hard work, and in particular to:

Liane Grainger and Lynn Townsend for supervising the whole project and guiding us calmly through the storms. Alison Bewsher for her keen editorial eye, enthusiasm and great suggestions.

Louise Wood for doing such a great job overseeing the level.

Liz Wilkie for her hard work and great editorial assistance.

We would also like to thank all our pupils and colleagues, past, present and future, at Star English academy in Murcia, especially Jim Kelly for his friendship and support throughout the years.

Dedications

For Alison Sharpe for seeing the potential, for Maria Pylas for driving it forward, for Susan Gonzalez for believing in and championing it, and for Liane Grainger for keeping us excellent, steadfast company throughout the whole of our stellar journey.

The authors and publishers acknowledge the following sources of copyright material and are grateful for the permissions granted. While every effort has been made; it has not always been possible to identify the sources of all the material used; or to trace all copyright holders. If any omissions are brought to our notice; we will be happy to include the appropriate acknowledgements on reprinting and in the next update to the digital edition; as applicable.

Key: U = Unit, V= Values

Photography

The following photos are sourced from Getty Images.

U0: brunorbs/iStock/Getty Images Plus; C Squared Studios/Photodisc; pagadesign/E+; studiocasper/E+; goir/iStock/Getty Images Plus; Dynamic Graphics Group; Peter Dazeley/The Image Bank; alexey_boldin/iStock/Getty Images Plus; Wattanaphob Kappago/EyeEm; frender/iStock/Getty Images Plus; davidf/iStock/Getty Images Plus; domin_domin/iStock/Getty Images Plus; UmbertoPantalone/iStock/Getty Images Plus; vectorshape/iStock/Getty Images Plus; Inside Creative House/iStock/Getty Images Plus; Cavan Images; JohnnyGreig/iStock/Getty Images Plus; Phynart Studio/E+; SDI Productions/E+; 'Volodymyr Kryshtal/iStock/Getty Images Plus; Tatiana Pankova/iStock/Getty Images Plus, 'kolotuschenko/iStock/Getty Images Plu, Nik01ay/iStock/Getty Images Plus; Tatiana Pankova/iStock/Getty Images Plus; Polina Tomtosova/iStock/Getty Images Plus; Chris Daborn/iStock/Getty Images Plus; gmm2000/iStock/Getty Images Plus U1: Glowimages; Jose Luis Pelaez Inc/DigitalVision; Aleksandr Zubkov/Moment; Anna Erastova/iStock/Getty Images Plus, Sussenn/iStock/Getty Images Plus; U2: Marko Geber/DigitalVision; Jonathan Knowles/Stone; Sigrid Gombert/Image Source; Ramberg/E+; 3DSculptor/iStock/Getty Images Plus; Space Frontiers/Archive Photos; R_Type/iStock/Getty Images Plus; Tara Moore/DigitalVision; GlinskajaOlga/iStock/Getty Images Plus; Panuwat Sikham/iStock/Getty Images Plus; bennyb/iStock/Getty Images Plus; Anna Erastova/iStock/Getty Images Plus; PeterSnow/iStock/Getty Images Plus; U3: Capuski/E+; adamkaz/E+; Suriyapong Thongsawang/Moment; Caia Image/Collection Mix Subjects; vgajic/E+; Ishii Koji/DigitalVision; lumpynoodles/DigitalVision Vectors; vectorsmarket/iStock/Getty Images Plus; Smashing Stocks/iStock/Getty Images Plus; JuliarStudio/iStock/Getty Images Plus; CasarsaGuru/E+; mgstudyo/iStock/Getty Images Plus; Arman Zhenikeyev/Corbis; Clive Brunskill/Getty Images Sport; FARBAI/iStock/Getty Images Plus; vav63/iStock/Getty Images Plus; Alina Ermokhina/iStock/Getty Images Plus; Good_Stock/iStock/Getty Images Plus; seamartini/iStock/Getty Images Plus; LizaLutik/iStock/Getty Images Plus; Anna Erastova/iStock/Getty Images Plus; U4: R.Tsubin/Moment; EasyBuy4u/iStock/Getty Images Plus; Kuzmik_A/iStock/Getty Images Plus; Nattawut Lakjit/EyeEm; Burazin/The Image Bank; Yevgen Romanenko/Moment; Tomas_Mina/iStock/Getty Images Plus; HEX; Morsa Images/DigitalVision; Richard Bailey/Corbis Documentary; Ana Silva/EyeEm; Maskot; Jonathan Kirn/The Image Bank; yalcinsonat1/iStock/Getty Images Plus; Ruta Lipskija/EyeEm; jayvo86/iStock/Getty Images Plus; irem01/iStock/Getty Images Plus; Tetiana Garkusha/iStock/Getty Images Plus; Michael Burrell/iStock/Getty Images Plus; akiyoko/iStock/Getty Images Plus; Rawf8/iStock/Getty Images Plus; Blackholy/iStock/Getty Images Plus; SGAPhoto/iStock/Getty Images Plus; urfinguss/iStock/Getty Images Plus; Elva Etienne/Moment; fleaz/iStock/Getty Images Plus; neyro2008/iStock/Getty Images Plus; LizaLutik/iStock/Getty Images Plus; Aleksangel/iStock/Getty Images Plus; golubovy/iStock/Getty Images Plus; Anna Erastova/iStock/Getty Images Plus; PeterSnow/iStock/Getty Images Plus; U5: VivianG/iStock/Getty Images Plus; Humberto Ramirez/Moment; Reinhard Dirscherl/The Image Bank; Gabrielle Yap/EyeEm; Raimundo Fernandez Diez/Moment; Andrew Peacock/Stone; by wildestanimal/Moment; piola666/E+; LUNAMARINA/iStock/Getty Images Plus; David Madison/DigitalVision; Patrick J. Endres/Corbis Documentary; evemilla/E+; CreativeI/iStock/Getty Images Plus; NadejdaReid/iStock/Getty Images Plus; standret/iStock/Getty Images Plus; Rhoberazzi/E+; S-S-S/iStock/Getty Images Plus; S-S-S/iStock/Getty Images Plus; LizaLutik/iStock/Getty Images Plus U6: Donald Iain Smith/Moment; sot/Photodisc; SDI Productions/E+; Jacobs Stock Photography Ltd/DigitalVision; Jupiterimages/Goodshoot; mediaphotos/iStock/Getty Images Plus; CasarsaGuru/E+; Tgordievskaya/iStock/Getty Images Plus; Robert Niedring/Cavan; Westend61; Mimi Haddon/DigitalVision; Nichola Sarah/Moment; Elva Etienne/Moment; Stefan Cristian Cioata/Moment; PraewBlackWhile/iStock/Getty Images Plus; Karen Brodie/Moment; Cezary Wojtkowski/iStock/Getty Images Plus; TomÃ¡s Pedreira/EyeEm; Hanna Plonsak/iStock/Getty Images Plus; CarlaNichiata/iStock/Getty Images Plus; Anna Erastova/iStock/Getty Images Plus; PeterSnow/iStock/Getty Images Plus; U7: Yura Yavorovich/iStock/Getty Images Plus; Klaus Hackenberg/The Image Bank; 10'000 Hours/DigitalVision BreakingTheWalls/iStock/Getty Images Plus; Joachim Berninger/EyeEm; Tom Baker/EyeEm; Helaine Weide/Moment; chris-mueller/iStock/Getty Images Plus; Katrin Ray Shumakov/Moment; YakubovAlim/iStock/Getty Images Plus; Jena Ardell/Moment; FatCamera/iStock/Getty Images Plus; NAKphotos/iStock/Getty Images Plus; Wavebreakmedia Ltd/Wavebreak Media; Lucidio Studio, Inc./Moment Open; Natalia-flurno/iStock/Getty Images Plus; Tetiana Lazunova/iStock/Getty Images Plus; Sentavio/iStock/Getty Images Plus; lukbar/iStock/Getty Images Plus; Anna Erastova/iStock/Getty Images Plus; Daria Pilshchikova/iStock/Getty Images Plus; Karuntana Chaiwatcharanun/iStock/Getty Images Plus; Maike Hildebrandt/iStock/Getty Images Plus; U8: Cultura RM Exclusive/Luc Beziat/Image Source; SDI Productions/E+; kali9/E+; xijian/E+; Caia Image/Collection Mix: Subjects; Siri Stafford/The Image Bank; Klaus Vedfelt/DigitalVision; stockvisual/E+; Iya Forbes/Moment; Jordan Lye/Moment; Yulia_Artemova/iStock/Getty Images Plus; seamartini/iStock/Getty Images Plus; Anna Erastova/iStock/Getty Images Plus; MuchMania/iStock/Getty Images Plus; PeterSnow/iStock/Getty Images Plus; Hanna Plonsak/iStock/Getty Images Plus; V82: Caia Image/Collection Mix: Subjects; V83: bortonia/DigitalVision Vectors; V84: Imgorthand/E+; Ryan McVay/DigitalVision; Studio Light and Shade/iStock/Getty Images Plus; Maskot; JGI/Jamie Grill/Tetra images; andresr/E+.

Cover photography by Tiffany Mumford for Creative Listening.

Commissioned photography by Stephen Noble and Duncan Yeldham for Creative Listening.

Illustrations

Ana Sebastian (Bright Agency); Dave Williams/Ryan Ball (roughs) (Bright Agency); David Belmont (Beehive); Javier Joaquin (Beehive); Laszlo Veres (Beehive); Moreno Chiacchiera (Beehive); Shahab (Sylvie Poggio).

Audio

Audio production by Sounds Like Mike Ltd.

Typeset

Blooberry Design

Additional authors

Rebecca Legros: CLIL
Montse Watkin: Sounds and Life Skills; Exam folder

Freelance editor

Melissa Bryant

Contents

⭐ **Smart technology** — 4

Sounds and life skills — 8

1 Beastly tales — 10

Sounds and life skills — 14
History: toys and games — 16
A2 Flyers: Listening Part 5 — 17

2 Tomorrow's world — 18

Sounds and life skills — 22
Physics: robots — 24
A2 Flyers: Reading and Writing Part 1 — 25
Review: units 1 and 2 — 26

3 The great outdoors — 28

Sounds and life skills — 32
Geography: mountains — 34
A2 Flyers: Listening Part 2 — 35

4 Food, glorious food! — 36

Sounds and life skills — 40
Biology: potatoes — 42
A2 Flyers: Reading and Writing Part 7 — 43
Review: units 3 and 4 — 44

5 Under the sea — 46

Sounds and life skills — 50
Environment: renewable energy — 52
A2 Flyers: Reading and Writing Part 2 — 53

6 Free time — 54

Sounds and life skills — 58
Design: rollercoasters — 60
A2 Flyers: Reading and Writing Part 3 — 61
Review: units 5 and 6 — 62

7 Fashion sense — 64

Sounds and life skills — 68
Design: fashion and the environment — 70
A2 Flyers: Listening Part 4 — 71

8 Around the world — 72

Sounds and life skills — 76
Maths: graphs and charts — 78
A2 Flyers: Reading and Writing Part 6 — 79
Review: units 7 and 8 — 80

⭐ **Values**

Values 1 & 2: living with technology — 82
Values 3 & 4: being safe at home — 83
Values 5 & 6: helping at home — 84
Values 7 & 8: sharing problems — 85
Grammar reference — 86
Irregular verbs — 88

1 Choose words from the box to complete the text.

> excited   going   horrible   laughed   maths
> something   ~~started~~   thirtieth   won   year

The children (1) ____started____ back at school last week and they're ready for another

(2) _____ of study. They're really (3) _____ about working on **Kid's Box** again,

their blog for young people. Last year they (4) _____ the school prize for the best project,

and this year they want to enter an international blog competition to see if they can win. They're

(5) _____ to visit lots of places and write about some very interesting things. Last

Wednesday they met to talk about their new project and they also looked at some funny photos from

last year. They (6) _____ a lot when they remembered some of the things that happened.

2 Correct the sentences.

1 The children started their holidays last week. <u>The children started back at school last week.</u>

2 They're ready for another month of study. _____

3 They won the school prize for art. _____

4 They met last Friday. _____

5 They watched some funny DVDs. _____

6 They cried a lot when they remembered. _____

3 What do you use these things for? Write sentences.

1   2   3

4   5   6

1 <u>We use a toothbrush to clean our teeth.</u>
2 _____
3 _____
4 _____
5 _____
6 _____

4 Answer the questions.

1 What did you do during the holidays?

_____

2 Where did you go?

_____

3 Who did you see?

_____

4 What did you eat?

_____

5 What did you do?

_____

6 Who were you with?

_____

Language: review of present tenses   ▶ Do the online activities on Practice Extra as you complete this unit

1 Put the words in groups.

bored English excited ~~friendly~~ geography history interested
~~maths~~ pepper ~~pizza~~ pleased salad salt sandwich science

friendly
___
___
___
___

pizza
___
___
___
___

maths
___
___
___
___

2 Find the letters on the clock. Make words.

1 It's twenty-five to twelve. ___wing___

2 It's twenty-five past six. ___

3 It's twenty to eleven. ___

4 It's ten past one. ___

5 It's ten to nine. ___

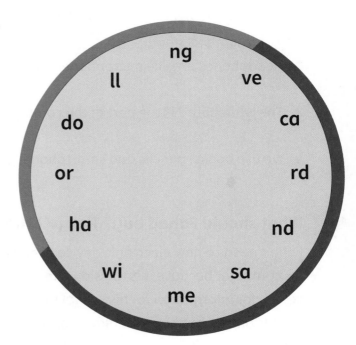

ng
ll   ve
do   ca
or   rd
ha   nd
wi   sa
me

3 Write times to make four more words. You can use the same letters again.

1 It's ten to eleven. (doll)

2 ___

3 ___

4 ___

4 Find and write the adjectives.

iped   ired   uge   errible   mous   orrible   ong   ~~mazing~~

amazing   h___   ngerous
a___   h___   t   rk
fa___   lo___   vely   potted
fa___   lo___   oft
da___   str___   ud
da___   str___   wake
s___   t___
s___   t___

Look and complete the words.

1 v <u>i d e o g a m e</u>

2 m _ _ _ _ _ _ p h _ _ _ _

3 e _ _ _ _ _ _

4 h _ _ _ _ _ p h _ _ _ _

5 l _ _ _ t _ _ _ _

6 s _ _ _ _ _ s p _ _ _ _ _ _

 Find the mistakes. Write the correct sentences.

1 A laptop is a big, heavy computer which we carry in a special bag.

   <u>A laptop is a small,</u> _____

2 Headphones are like microphones. We use them to see our friends when we chat with them.

   _____

3 The whiteboard is the part of the computer we look at. We use it to watch videos.

   _____

4 We use books, pencils and smartphones to connect with people and programmes online.

   _____

 What should Fahad buy? Tick (✓) the correct box.

Fahad needs a new electronic device because his computer is very old. He has a lot of problems with his computer because it is too slow. He wants a fast internet connection because he often needs to search for information for his school projects and upload his homework. He also likes to chat with his friends online, but he never plays games. He wants an electronic device he can carry when he travels which can take photos and videos. The screen needs to be a large size to look at the photos and videos. He also wants a keyboard which is easy to use and isn't very small.

4 📝 **Write three reasons why you chose that electronic device in your notebook.**

1 Join two words to make one. Write the new word.

1	home	ball	_____
2	head	line	_____
3	on	room	_____
4	class	work	_homework_
5	basket	phones	_____

2 Write another word at the end to make new words.

1 bath<u>room</u>   3 ear_____   5 arm_____   7 foot_____

2 book_____   4 hand_____   6 tooth_____   8 snow_____

3 Find and say eight differences. Then write sentences.

In picture a, the girl's chatting online. In picture b, she's watching a film.

_____

_____

_____

_____

_____

_____

_____

4 Answer the questions.

1 How do you go online? _____

2 Do you write emails? _____

3 Do you use apps to chat with your friends? _____

4 Have you got a smart speaker at home? _____

5 Do you upload your homework to an app? _____

6 Do you play online video games with your friends? _____

7 How do you listen to music? _____

8 Do you prefer laptops, tablets or smartphones? _____

Sounds and life skills
Being a good school citizen
Pronunciation focus

1 **Listen and circle the stressed part of the words.**

1 compe(ti)tion
2 computer
3 exciting
4 internet

5 laptop
6 tablet
7 technology

2 **Complete with the words from Activity 1. Listen and check.**

1 Oo	2 Ooo	3 oOo	4 oOoo	5 ooOo
				competition

3 **Listen and number the pictures.**

a

b

c 1

d

e

4 **Read and complete.** arrive ~~change~~ do help keep look

How to be a good school citizen

We have to …

change our library books every week.
_____ at class on time.
_____ our classroom tidy.

_____ our classmates.
_____ our homework.
_____ after the technology we use.

Sounds and life skills: stressed words | social responsibility

Read and answer.

Diggory Bones

1 What time's Diggory giving his talk? At half past two.
2 What kind of computer has Diggory got? _____
3 What can he use to explain ancient maths and technology? _____
4 Who's Sir Doug Bones? _____
5 Why does he want to look under the cloth? _____
6 Who's got the calendar at the end? _____

 Look at the code. Write the secret message.

a	b	c	d	e	f	g	h	i	j	k	l	m

n	o	p	q	r	s	t	u	v	w	x	y	z

T h e _____ _____ _____ _____

_____ _____ _____ _____ _____ _____ _____

Do you remember?

1 10.55 is five _____ to _____ eleven.
2 _____ don't we buy a new computer?
3 I play online _____ with my friends all over the world.
4 A small computer which we can carry easily is a _____ .
5 _____ and _____ are two words with the stress pattern Oo.
6 One word with the stress pattern oOoo is _____ .

Can do

I can make and agree to suggestions.   ☹   ☺   ☺

I can talk about technology.   ☹   ☺   ☺

I can write about my school.   ☹   ☺   ☺

1 Beastly tales

We use *going to* to talk about plans.

Affirmative	Negative	Question
I'm **going to** read.	You **aren't going to** listen to music.	**Is** he **going to** play tennis?
She's **going to** read.	We **aren't going to** listen to music.	**Are** they **going to** play tennis?
We're **going to** read.	He **isn't going to** listen to music.	**Am** I **going to** play tennis?

1 Correct the questions and answer.

1 Am you going to be in the school play? Are you going to be in the school play? No, I'm not.
2 Do your dad going to cook dinner tonight? _____
3 Are you go to watch a film after school? _____
4 Has your mum going to the theatre this weekend? _____
5 What is your friends going to do at the weekend? _____
6 Does your teacher going to give you homework today? _____

2 Complete the questions. Match them with the answers.

> What   When   Where   ~~Which~~   Who   Why

1 __Which__ bus are you going to catch?
2 _____ are we going to play football?
3 _____ is he going to call?
4 _____ is she going to wash the car?
5 _____ is he going to read?
6 _____ are they going to do the exam?

a He's going to call his mum. ☐
b They're going to do it tomorrow. ☐
c He's going to read his comic. ☐
d I'm going to catch the number 27. ☐ 1
e In the park. ☐
f Because it's dirty. ☐

3 Look at the code. Write the secret message.

H	I	J	K	L	M	N	O	P	Q	R	S	T	U	V	W	X	Y	Z	A	B	C	D	E	F	G
A	B	C	D	E	F	G	H	I	J	K	L	M	N	O	P	Q	R	S	T	U	V	W	X	Y	Z

A O L   A O L H A Y L   J S B I   P Z   N V P U N   A V   Z O V D   A O L   W S H F
T h e ___ ___ ___ ___ ___ ___ ___ ___ ___ ___ ___ ___ ___ ___ ___ ___ ___ ___ ___ ___ ___ ___ ___ ___ ___ ___ ___ ___ ___

V U   A O L   S H Z A   A O B Y Z K H F   H U K   M Y P K H F   V M   Q B U L .
___ ___ ___ ___ ___ ___ ___ ___ ___ ___ ___ ___ ___ ___ ___ ___ ___ ___ ___ ___ ___ ___ ___ ___ ___ ___ ___ ___ ___ ___ ___ ___ ___ .

Language: plans, intentions and predictions with *going to*   Do the online activities on **Practice Extra** as you complete this unit

1 **Find six sentences or questions and write them in your notebook.**

He isn't	tickets do you	animals.
How many	to get parts in	tomorrow.
Are they going	going to be	monkey.
They didn't	isn't going to rain	an actor.
Lions	choose him for the	the play?
It	catch and eat	want?

2 **What are they going to do?**

1 Hiroto's switching on the TV.
   He's going to watch TV.

2 Lola's standing outside the castle and she's holding her camera.

   _____

3 The car's very dirty. Mr White is walking towards it with some water.

   _____

4 Some people are standing at the bus stop.

   _____

5 The boys are walking to the park. They're carrying a football.

   _____

6 There's some paper in front of Petra and she's picking up a pen.

   _____

3 **Think about next year. Write notes to answer the questions.**

1 How old are you going to be? _____
2 What class are you going to be in at school? _____
3 Which subjects are you going to study? _____
4 Which clubs are you going to join? _____
5 What are you going to do after school and on which days? _____
6 Which books are you going to read? _____
7 Which films are you going to see? _____
8 What else are you going to do? _____

4 **Use your answers to write sentences about what you're going to do next year.**

In January next year, I'm going to be _____

1 Find the words. Label the picture.

f	a	i	r	i	e	n
n	e	s	t	o	s	h
a	a	a	u	e	c	o
o	g	g	t	e	a	r
e	l	a	o	h	l	n
f	e	e	o	u	e	f
c	l	a	w	u	s	r

1 _____eagle_____

2 _____

3 _____

4 _____

5 _____

6 _____

 2 Look at the picture and correct the sentences.

1 The dragon's got fur on its body. _The dragon's got scales on its body._

2 The dragon wants to get the parrot's eggs. _____

3 The dragon and the eagle have got dangerous hands. _____

4 The dragon's got feathers on its wings, but the eagle hasn't. _____

5 The dragon's got two ears on its head. _____

6 The eagle's eggs are in a cave. _____

 3 Look at these beasts. Invent names and describe them.

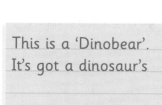

This is a 'Dinobear'.
It's got a dinosaur's

Read and answer 'yes' or 'no'.

The Sphinx existed in ancient Egyptian and ancient Greek mythology. In Greek mythology the Sphinx had a lion's body, legs and claws, a snake's tail, eagle's wings and a woman's head. The story says that she sat at the door of the ancient city of Thebes to guard it. To go into the city people had to answer the Sphinx's question. If they got it right, they could go into the city. If they got it wrong, she ate them. The Ancient Greek writer, Sophocles, wrote the question in his work. It was 'Which creature goes on four feet in the morning, two feet in the afternoon and three feet in the evening?' Do you know the answer?

1 The Sphinx was a real animal. ___no___
2 She had a bird's wings. _____
3 She had a mammal's tail. _____

4 She stood at the door of Thebes. _____
5 She asked people a question. _____
6 People who didn't know went home. _____

2 **Write the words.**

1 an ancient story about heroes = ___myth___
2 snakes have got these on their bodies = _____
3 birds have got these on their wings = _____
4 a word for an animal or creature = _____
5 a very expensive yellow metal = _____
6 some birds make these in trees = _____
7 the home of a king or queen = _____
8 half woman, half fish = _____

3 **What's going to happen?**

The boat is going to break
on the rocks. _____ _____

_____ _____ _____

Sounds and life skills

Supporting your friends

Pronunciation focus

1 🎧 5 **Listen and write.**   1 r _ _ _   3 p _ _ _   5 _____   7 _____
2 b r _ _ _   4 w _ _ _   6 _____

2 🎧 6 **Listen and complete. Practise saying the sentences.**

> acting   exciting   going   interesting   ~~singing~~   starting   Writing

1 I'm good at _____singing_____ but I'm not good at _____.
2 I love _____ to the theatre!
3 I'm _____ a new course after school today.
4 I think dragons are _____ but they're also a bit scary.
5 _____ a blog isn't always easy but it's _____.

3 **Read and match.**

1 I'm worried about my exams
2 I'm starting a sailing course
3 I'm good at singing on stage
4 I'm going to play in my first football match

a but I'm terrible at scoring goals.
b but I get very nervous in front of a lot of people.
c because I get very nervous and forget things!
d and I'm worried because I'm not a strong swimmer.

4 **Read and complete the advice. Then match with a situation in Activity 3.**

> can   Go   good   luck   Well   ~~worry~~

a Don't _____worry_____. You're _____ at singing! Close your eyes and enjoy the songs! ☐

b You're on holiday! Why not start a swimming course at the same time? _____ for it! ☐

c It's fantastic you are on the football team! _____ done! Practise scoring your goals with a friend at the weekend. ☐

d You _____ do it! Talk about the topic with a friend or your family. Relax and go to bed early the night before. Good _____! ☐

1 Read and answer.

Diggory Bones

1 Where's the Aztec calendar from? <u>It's from a museum in Mexico City.</u>
2 Who's Iyam Greedy? _____
3 How do you write 6 in the Mayan maths system? _____
4 Who was Quetzalcoatl? _____
5 What's in the email? _____
6 Where are Diggory and Emily going to go? _____

2 Complete and match.

1 How am I ___going to___ tell the museum in Mexico City? **d**

2 A spot means one and _____ five.

3 It _____ a phone number to me.

4 I'm a snake and I _____ .

5 He was _____ and part snake.

 a
 b
 c
 d
 e

Do you remember?

1 They aren't ___going___ to choose Stella for the part of the monkey.
2 They are going _____ write about exciting beasts.
3 Dragons have got _____ on their bodies.
4 Eagles live in _____ in high places.
5 _____ is the day before Friday and the day after Wednesday.
6 There are _____ days in the weekend.

Can do

I can talk about what is going to happen.
I can talk about beasts from myths and legends.
I can write about mythical beasts.

How have our toys and games changed?

1 Read and complete with 'who' and 'which'.

Everybody loves

Leslie Scott is the name of the British board-game designer (1) _____who_____ created Jenga in the 1970s. The game begins with a tower (2) _____ has 54 blocks. Players must take the blocks away from the tower without making it fall, and then put the blocks on the top.

The game needs two or more players. The winner is the player (3) _____ does not make the tower fall over. It's a game (4) _____ takes between five and 15 minutes to play.

The name Jenga comes from **kujenga**, a Swahili word (5) _____ means 'to build'.

Jenga is a game without a board, and I believe that everyone (6) _____ loves board games will also love Jenga!

2 Plan to write a review. Complete the table for a game you enjoy.

My Review	
Paragraph 1 What's the game?	_____ is a _____ game which _____. The winner is the player who _____.
Paragraph 2 How do you play the game?	The game has got _____. Players use _____ to _____. It's a game which usually takes _____ minutes.
Paragraph 3 How many players do you need?	To play _____, you need _____ players. Players should be aged between _____. This makes it a perfect game for _____.
Paragraph 4 What do you think?	I believe every house should have _____ because _____.

3 ✍ Use your notes to write your game review.

4 Did you …

- ☐ plan your game review?
- ☐ use interesting words to describe the game?
- ☐ give your own opinion?
- ☐ read your game review again?
- ☐ check grammar, spelling and punctuation?

Writing tip

Writing a game review

When you write a game review, you should give some facts about the game, but you can also say what you like and what you don't like.

Cluedo is a game **which** …

I think Cluedo is a great game because …

1 🎧 7 **Listen and colour and write. There is one example.**

2 Tomorrow's world

will

We use *will* to talk about the future.

Affirmative	Negative	Question
I'**ll** go to the moon.	You **won't** travel by car.	**Will** she fly in a rocket?
It'**ll** go to the moon.	We **won't** travel by car.	**Will** they fly in a rocket?

1 Read and match.

1 We will have
2 She won't go
3 He will go to
4 There won't be any
5 Someone will
6 Some people

a invent a carplane. ☐
b will go to the moon on holiday. ☐
c online classes every day. ☐ 1
d work by rocket. ☐
e to school by bus. ☐
f cars in a hundred years. ☐

2 Complete the table. Tick (✓) 'Yes' or 'No'.

Will you ...	Yes	No
1 travel to the Moon?		
2 have the same job as your parents?		
3 have lots of pets?		
4 live in the same town as you live in now?		
5 go to university when you're older?		

3 Now write sentences with 'will' or 'won't'.

I will / won't travel to the moon.

1 _____
2 _____
3 _____
4 _____
5 _____

4 Read the notes. Complete the sentences.

9.00	Arrive at school. Change clothes for sports lesson.
9.15	Play badminton.
10.00	Have a shower.
10.30	Go to maths lesson.
11.15	Go out to play. Drink some orange juice.

1 When Peter arrives at school, he'll change his clothes for sport _____ .

2 After he plays badminton, _____ _____ .

3 After he has maths, _____ _____ .

4 When he goes out to play, _____ _____ .

⟐ Do the online activities on Practice Extra as you complete this unit

1 **Will these things happen in 2075? Write sentences with 'will' or 'won't'.**

1 Children / classes / home <u>Children won't have classes at home.</u>

2 People / go / Mars _____

3 People / fly / cars _____

4 People / use smartphones _____

5 Children / do sports outside _____

6 People / use less plastic _____

2 **Read and complete.**

arms   cup   clean   quickly   ~~shower~~   will   won't

This is my new invention to help children in the future. It's a cross between a (1) __shower__ and a car-wash. It'll have two funny metal (2) _____ with big gloves made of rubber. These (3) _____ move round and round very (4) _____ to wash us with soap and water. One of them will (5) _____ our teeth with a toothbrush too. Outside the shower there'll be a machine with an engine to dry us. It'll look like a big (6) _____ which we'll stand under. We'll have a shower and we (7) _____ have a wet towel.

3 **Design and draw an invention to help children in the future.**

4 **Write about your invention.**

1 Label the photos.

astronaut   business person   Earth   engineer   rocket   ~~tourist~~

tourist

_____

_____

_____

_____

_____

2 Complete the sentences.

1 _____Space_____ is the name we give to everything outside Earth's air.

2 An _____ is a person who designs or makes machines or electrical things.

3 We breathe _____ .

4 The planet _____ is where we live.

5 An _____ can travel in space.

6 The _____ goes round our planet. We can see it at night.

7 A _____ visits another town or country on holiday.

8 Someone who works in business is called a _____ .

9 A _____ goes very quickly and can take people into space.

3 Read and answer 'yes' or 'no'.

The Space Race started in 1957 when the Soviet Union sent a satellite called Sputnik 1 into space. A satellite is something which goes round Earth. The USA sent a satellite, called Explorer 1, into space in 1958. Eleven years later, the American astronaut Neil Armstrong became the first person to walk on the moon. Now, we can explore further into space with robots instead of people. In July 2020, NASA sent a big robot called Perseverance to Mars. It carried a small helicopter with it to take photos. Mars is very far away from Earth. Perseverance didn't land on Mars until February 2021!

1 The first satellite in space was called Sputnik 1. _yes_

2 The USA sent a satellite into space in 1959. _____

3 Neil Armstrong was the first man to walk on the moon. _____

4 NASA sent astronauts to Mars in 2020. _____

5 Perseverance took a small helicopter with it. _____

6 Perseverance landed on Mars in 2020. _____

1 Match the ideas about life on Zeron, the space city. Write sentences.

1 telescopes in the windows
2 satellites
3 solar panels
4 robots
5 rockets

a to build new houses
b to get energy
c to travel into space
d to look at the stars
e to receive signals from space

☐
☐
☐
1
☐

1 We'll have telescopes in the windows to look at the stars.
2 _____
3 _____
4 _____
5 _____

2 Read and answer the riddles.

1 The beginning of Earth, the end of space. The beginning of every end, the end of every place. What am I? _____ 'e' _____

2 What comes once in a minute, twice in a moment, and never in a thousand years? _____

3 Which letter will come next in this sequence? M, A, M, J, J, A, S, O … ? _____

4 How will you use the letters in NEW DOOR to make one word? _____

5 Akash was an engineer. His mother had four children. The first was April, the second was May and the third was June. What was the name of her fourth child? _____

6 A man's looking at a photo of a famous astronaut and he says, 'I have no brothers and sisters, but that man's father is my father's son.' Who's he looking at? _____

3 Read and complete the circle with names and jobs.

There are three girls and two boys. They're talking about the jobs they think they will (✓) and won't (✗) do in the future.

1 Petra's sitting between Quinn and Lucas. The person on Lucas's left thinks she'll be an actor but she won't be a painter.

2 The boy who says he'll be a dentist won't be an actor.

3 The person on Mary's left won't be a photographer but she thinks she'll be a mechanic.

4 The girl next to Lucy loves cameras so she'll be a photographer, but she won't be a cook.

5 The boy next to Lucy loves rockets but he won't be an astronaut. He thinks he'll be a rocket engineer.

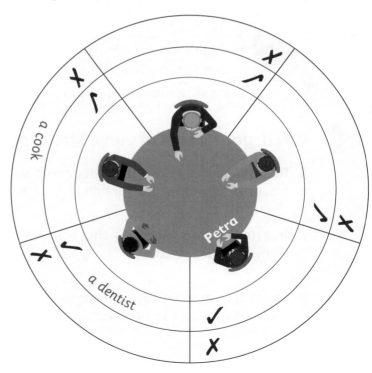

Sounds and life skills
Choosing a point of view

Pronunciation focus

1 8 **Listen and underline the stress in the verbs.**

In 2100 …

1 People will <u>travel</u> to the moon on holiday.
2 School trips will visit space.
3 We'll ride bicycles that can fly.

4 Students won't have paper coursebooks.
5 Everyone will wear a computer on their arm.
6 People won't shop at supermarkets.

2 **Read the rules and circle 'weak' or 'strong'.**

We don't say every word in a sentence with the same stress. The strong words give important information. When we make the important words stronger, it's easier for people to understand.

1 Verbs, adjectives and nouns are usually **weak / strong**.

2 Helping verbs (**will, can, should**) are usually **weak / strong**.

3 Negative words (**won't, don't, didn't**) are usually **weak / strong**.

> We'll **travel** by **fast cars**, but they **won't** use **petrol**.

3 9 **Listen. What does Nico think? Tick (✓) 'Agree' or 'Disagree'.**

	Agree	Disagree
1 moon holidays	✓	
2 school trips to space		
3 flying bicycles		
4 no paper coursebooks		
5 computers on arms		
6 no supermarket shopping		

4 **Circle your point of view. Then complete with a reason.**

1 In 2100, I **agree / disagree** that people will travel to the moon for their holidays because

_____.

2 In 2100, I **agree / disagree** that school trips will visit space because

_____.

3 In 2100, I **agree / disagree** that we'll ride bicycles that can fly because

_____.

4 In 2100, I **agree / disagree** that students won't have paper coursebooks because

_____.

5 In 2100, I **agree / disagree** that everyone will wear a computer on their arm because

_____.

6 In 2100, I **agree / disagree** that people won't shop at supermarkets because

_____.

1 Read and answer.

Diggory Bones

1 Why did Iyam Greedy send them tickets to Mexico City? <u>There are legends about Aztec gold.</u>
2 What did the Aztecs and the Mayas use to measure time? _____
3 When did the Aztec new year start? _____
4 What will be the longest day of the year? _____
5 What's the date now in the story? _____
6 Will they stay in Mexico City tonight? _____

2 📝 Read and order the text. Write the story in your notebook.

technology and their ancient maths system. Iyam Greedy, who's a pirate and ☐

notebook and talked about a group of stars. There was a man sitting next to them. He ☐

phone number for Diggory in a letter. When Diggory phoned the number, Iyam ☐

only wants to get the Aztec gold and be rich, stole the Sun Stone and left a ☐

Diggory Bones is an archaeologist who teaches at City University. He had the ☐ 1

On the plane to Mexico City, Diggory and his daughter, Emily, looked at a ☐

man from the plane got into a car with Iyam Greedy and followed their bus. ☐

listened to them talking. When Diggory and Emily caught a bus to Teotihuacan, the ☐

talked about Aztec mythology. Then he sent him two plane tickets in an email. ☐

Sun Stone. This is the name for the Aztec calendar, which he had to talk about Mayan (and Aztec) ☐

Do you remember?

1 In the future there ____will____ be spaceplanes.
2 That's not a very good paper plane. It _____ fly very far.
3 _____ are people who fly in space in their job.
4 Our planet is called _____ .
5 In the question 'When'll they arrive?', ''ll' is a contraction of _____ .
6 _____ they build a spaceplane for tourists, we'll fly round Earth on our holiday.

Can do

I can talk about what will happen. ☹ ☺ 😀
I can talk about travel in the future. ☹ ☺ 😀
I can write about how we'll live in the future. ☹ ☺ 😀

What can robots do for us?

1 Read and order. Then circle the instruction verbs.

MY SCHOOL PROJECT

Draw a simple design of your robot. Decide which materials you will need. `[1]`

Finally, colour the robot's body and decorate its face. `[ ]`

Test the robot to check it won't break. `[ ]`

Build your robot with the materials. `[ ]`

Find the materials you need to build your robot. `[ ]`

2 Plan to write instructions. Complete the table about how to make a robot. Use the instruction verbs from the box.

> Bring   build   Choose   ~~decide~~   decorate   Draw   Paint   plan   Write

Type of robot	How to make a _____.
Instructions	First, ____decide____ what type of robot to make.
	Then _____ your robot. Think about what it will look like and what you will need.
	_____ a picture of what your robot will look like.
	_____ the materials you will need. _____ them down in your notebook.
	Now _____ your robot carefully with your materials. If something doesn't work, try again!
	_____ and _____ your robot with colours. Look at your picture again to help you.
	_____ your robot to school and show your friends!

3 Use your notes to write your instructions.

4 Did you …

- [ ] plan your instructions?
- [ ] use instruction verbs?
- [ ] read your instructions again?
- [ ] check grammar, spelling and punctuation?

Writing tip

Writing instructions

Instructions should start with the first thing you need to do. They should finish with the last thing you need to do. Use words like **choose, plan, draw, build, paint** and **colour** to show how to make something.

Physics: robots | creative thinking

Flyers Reading and Writing Part 1

1 **Look and read. Choose the correct words and write them on the lines. There is one example.**

rockets   a monkey   a theatre   stars

	You use this to take photos. It isn't a smartphone.	_a camera_

~~a camera~~   **1** A big road where people can drive fast.   _____   a lion

2 Astronauts use these to fly into space.   _____

3 This is a person who flies a plane.   _____

a mouse   **4** This day comes after Wednesday.   _____   an island

5 This animal is a very big cat. It's called 'The King of the Beasts'.   _____

planets   **6** This is a piece of land in the sea. There's water all around it.   _____   a driver

7 This is the place where you go to see a play.   _____

8 There are a lot of these in the sky. You can see them clearly at night.   _____

gold   **9** There are eight of these in our solar system.   _____   **a stadium**

10 This yellow metal is very expensive. People make rings and bracelets from it.   _____

a pilot   Thursday   **trees**   a motorway

1 **Read the story. Choose a word from the box. Write the correct word next to numbers 1–8.**

> actor   cook   designer   drive   engineer   ~~favourite~~   food
> future   house   museum   picture   rocket   tomorrow   will   won't

FRIENDLY

Friendly is Stella, Meera and Lenny's ___favourite___ TV programme. It's a comedy and it's very funny. It's about five friends who all live and study in the same school. Last week the friends had an interview with a special teacher to talk about their (1) _____ jobs. They had to think about which school subjects they were good at, and where they wanted to work.

Frankie wants to study art at university. Jim loves sport and keeping fit and wants to be a fire fighter. Peter loves (2) _____ and he says he'll be a cook. Sally says she'll be a taxi driver. Jenny's good at English and drama and wants to be an (3) _____. She says that when she's famous, Sally (4) _____ drive her to the film studio, Peter will (5) _____ her lovely meals and Frankie will paint her a (6) _____ and put it in a big, important (7) _____. When Jim asks what he'll do for her, Jenny says her (8) _____ will never catch fire so he'll have to change his job!

2 **Now choose the best name for the story.**

Tick one box.   Past and present   ☐   After-school club   ☐   Future plans   ☐

3 **Read and match the jokes.**

1 What's green and smells like paint?	**a** The outside.
2 How does a monster count to 13?	**b** All of them can. A house can't jump.
3 Which side of an eagle has the most feathers?	**c** A purple carrot!
4 What do you get if you cross a blue cat with a red parrot?	**d** I don't know, but when it talks you should listen carefully!
5 How many seconds are there in a year?	**e** Green paint.
6 Which animal can jump higher than a house?	**f** On its fingers!
7 Where can you find a sea without water?	**g** A road.
8 Why don't mother kangaroos like rainy days?	**h** On a map!
9 What goes through towns and up and over hills, but doesn't move?	**i** Twelve: January the second, February the second …
10 What do you get if you cross a parrot with a tiger?	**j** Because their children have to play inside!

Answer boxes:
1 (second box), e → 1

4 Complete the sentences. Count and write the letters.

1 _____Space_____ is the place outside Earth's air, where the moon and planets are. ⑤

2 A griffin's nest is made of _____ . ☐

3 Wi-Fi, smart speakers, TVs, headphones and the internet are all examples of _____ . ☐

4 We breathe _____ . It's called 'wind' when it moves over Earth. ☐

5 Somebody who works in space is an _____ . ☐

6 Eagles have got lots of _____ on their wings. ☐

7 A small, light computer that we can carry easily is a _____ . ☐

8 'What _____ you do?' 'I'll ask Hiroto to help me.' ☐

9 The sun is the only _____ in our solar system. ☐

10 The _____ is the part of the computer which has the letters which we use to write. ☐

11 A space station uses a _____ to send astronauts into space. ☐

12 An _____ designs cars and motorbikes. ☐

13 We send an _____ to our friends using the internet. ☐

14 _____ are at the end of a dragon's leg. ☐

5 Now complete the crossword. Write the message.

(crossword grid)

1 2 3 4   5 6   7 8 9 10
☐☐☐☐ ☐☐ ☐☐☐ s !

6 Quiz time!

1 What part did Stella play in the audition? The naughty monkey.

2 Who did Jason sail with? _____

3 Where did people play Senet? _____

4 How will tourists fly into space in the future? _____

5 What do astronauts need to live in space for a long time? _____

6 How fast can Raptor the robot run? _____

7 ✎ Write questions for your quiz in your notebook.

Review: units 1 and 2   27

3 The great outdoors

We use the past continuous to describe what was happening in the past.

Affirmative	Negative	Question
I **was climbing** when I fell.	I **wasn't walking**.	**Was** I **playing**?
You **were climbing** when you fell.	He **wasn't walking**.	**Was** she **playing**?
He **was climbing** when he fell.	They **weren't walking**.	**Were** we **playing**?

 Read and match.

1 She was skating
2 We were cooking sausages
3 You were flying your kite
4 He was skiing down the hill fast
5 I was sleeping
6 They were waiting at the station

when

a he saw a tree in front of him.
b it flew into a tree.
c she fell down.
d the kitchen caught fire.
e their train arrived.
f you phoned me.

☐
☐
☐ 1
☐
☐
☐

 Look at the pictures. Answer the questions.

1 Was Richard playing volleyball at quarter past eleven? <u>Yes, he was.</u>
2 Were Tanaz and George doing their homework at quarter past five? _____
3 Was Hiroto playing the guitar at ten past seven? _____
4 Were Kito and Yu Xi having lunch at twenty-five past one? _____
5 Was Sophia cleaning her teeth at half past eight? _____
6 Were Nadia and Oliver watching TV at ten to five? _____

 Complete the sentences for you.

1 Yesterday I was going to school when _____
2 When I was eating my breakfast this morning _____
3 My friends were playing at the weekend when _____
4 When our teacher was talking _____

Language: past continuous and past simple   ▸ Do the online activities on **Practice Extra** as you complete this unit

1 Match the sentences with the pictures.

1 We looked at our map. We had to walk through a forest to get to the campsite.

2 In this picture we were eating the sandwiches which George and Harry got from the café. We couldn't eat the sausages because they burned black!

3 Last week I went camping with my friends George and Harry. When we got off the bus, it was raining.

4 Our feet were hurting after the long walk and we were tired and hungry when we arrived.

5 It was getting late when we were walking through the forest and it was very dark.

6 This is a picture of me when I was cooking the sausages. I'm not a very good cook.

2 Read and answer 'yes' or 'no'.

1 He went camping with his friends Harry and George. _yes_

2 It was raining when they got off the bus. _____

3 They had to walk up a hill to get to the campsite. _____

4 The Sun was coming up when they were walking through the forest. _____

5 Their feet were hurting when they arrived at the campsite. _____

6 When he was cooking the sausages, he burned them. _____

3 Read and answer.

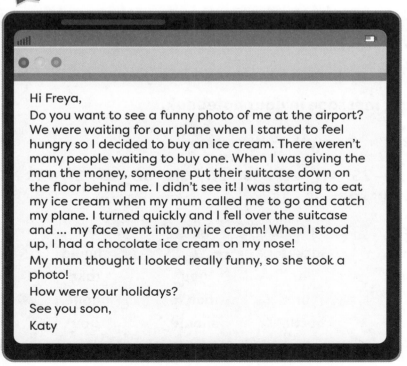

Hi Freya,

Do you want to see a funny photo of me at the airport? We were waiting for our plane when I started to feel hungry so I decided to buy an ice cream. There weren't many people waiting to buy one. When I was giving the man the money, someone put their suitcase down on the floor behind me. I didn't see it! I was starting to eat my ice cream when my mum called me to go and catch my plane. I turned quickly and I fell over the suitcase and … my face went into my ice cream! When I stood up, I had a chocolate ice cream on my nose!

My mum thought I looked really funny, so she took a photo!

How were your holidays?

See you soon,

Katy

1 What were Katy and her mum doing in the airport? They were waiting for the plane.

2 Were there many people waiting to buy an ice cream? _____

3 When did someone put their suitcase down behind her? _____

4 What was she starting to do when her mum called her? _____

5 What did her mum think when she stood up? _____

Language: past continuous and past simple   29

1 Look at the picture. Find the words a–l in the wordsearch.

s	o	o	p	d	r	o	h	r	y
l	e	r	f	n	c	w	e	s	t
e	b	c	e	o	n	t	k	t	g
e	a	h	e	s	r	n	o	s	h
p	c	s	n	k	t	e	n	t	i
i	t	a	t	a	z	y	s	a	l
n	o	e	m	p	n	r	e	t	l
g	r	e	x	p	l	o	r	e	r
b	c	s	q	i	u	g	r	l	a
a	h	t	n	x	s	o	u	t	h
g	r	u	c	k	s	a	c	k	h

2 Write the words. Then write the letters from Activity 1.

1 _____camp_____ = to live and sleep outdoors ☐ a

2 _____ = a bag you can sleep in ☐

3 _____ = the opposite of north ☐

4 _____ = something you can use to see when it's dark ☐

5 _____ = a high place that's lower than a mountain ☐

6 _____ = a place where you can sleep ☐

3 Write definitions for three more words in Activity 1. Then write the letters.

_____ ☐

_____ ☐

_____ ☐

4 Look at the code. Write the secret message in your notebook.

> N = north   E = east   S = south   W = west

When – 5E – 4N – 2W – 3S – 2W – 1N – 3E – 2S – 4N – 2W – 3S – 2W – 2N – 5E – 1S – 2W – 2S – 2W – 1E – 2N – 2W – 2N – 1E – 1S – 2E – 1W – 2E – 2S – 1E.

a	warm,	carry	walking	always	are
You	dry	and	jacket	a	should
fruit,	hills,	some	a	you	take
rucksack.	the	a	in	mobile	phone.
When	of	water,	bottle	should	you

Read the sentences. Draw and write on the map.

 The New Forest is 5 km north of Starton.

 The hills are 3 km east of the New Forest.

 There's a bridge over the river 5 km west of the New Forest.

 2 km south of the hills there's a hotel. Its name is the Happy Inn.

 There's a lake 5 km west of Starton. It's called Windymere.

 Old Hampton is 2 km north of Windymere.

 The campsite is 3 km east of Old Hampton.

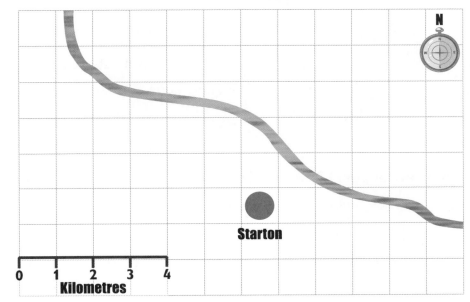

Starton

0   1   2   3   4
Kilometres

 Now draw these things on the map in Activity 1. Write the directions.

The torch is _____ .

The rucksack is _____ .

The umbrella is _____ .

The suitcase is _____ .

 Find the letters on the clock. Write the words.

1 It's quarter to eight.   _____south_____

2 It's five past ten.   _____

3 It's twenty-five past eight. _____

4 It's quarter past six.   _____

5 It's twenty past ten.   _____

 Write times to make four more words in your notebook.

Sounds and life skills
Imagining possibilities
Pronunciation focus

1 🎧 10 **Listen and write the words under /b/, /v/ or /w/.**

/b/	/v/	/w/
bridge		

2 🎧 11 **Complete with words from Activity 1. Listen and check.**

1 Look! There's a _____ bike _____ on the _____ !

2 Let's _____ in the _____ . It's a beautiful day.

3 Why don't we _____ a _____ ? It's very cold outside.

4 We always _____ my aunt Vicky on Wednesdays.

5 Oh no! My _____ fell in the river _____ we were looking at the _____ !

3 🎧 12 **Order the sentences. Listen and check.**

1 walking / river / fast / We / were / over a / when I fell in.
   We were walking over a fast river when I fell in.

2 walking / bridge / were / We / on a / when I fell and broke my leg.
   _____

3 big / were / in a / We / wood / walking / when I broke my leg.
   _____

4 near a / beautiful / walking / were / We / waterfall / when I fell in.
   _____

4 **How did they break their arm? Look and complete.** (jump   ride   run)

1 I was _____ when I broke my arm!

2 _____ when I broke my arm!

3 _____ when I broke my arm!

1 Read and answer.

Diggory Bones

1 Who was getting out of the car behind them? Richard Tricker was getting out of the car.
2 Where's the Temple of Quetzalcoatl? _____
3 How far is Mexico City from the hotel? _____
4 Why does the man know about this place? _____
5 What does the long street join? _____
6 Was Diggory expecting to see Iyam there? _____

2 Put the verbs into the past.

The story of Mexico City
In about 1325 some young Aztec men (1) __were getting__ (are getting) food for their people when they
(2) _____ (see) an eagle. It (3) _____ (is sitting) on a plant which
(4) _____ (is growing) on a rock in the middle of a lake called Texcoco.
They (5) _____ (think) it (6) _____ (is) a special sign and they (7)_____
(decide) to build their city there.

The Aztecs (8) _____ (are) great engineers. They (9) _____ (take) the water away
from the lake to make the island bigger. They (10) _____ (build) canals so people
(11) _____ (can) move around the city by boat, and bridges which they (12) _____
(take) away at night to protect their city. They (13) _____ (call) their city Tenochtitlan and it
(14) _____ (become) one of the biggest and most important cities in the world at that time.
The Aztecs (15) _____ (are) very rich because they (16) _____ (have) land, farms,
markets and shops. They (17) _____ (use) the Mayan number system and calendar and they
(18) _____ (study) the stars and the night sky carefully. Like the Ancient Egyptians, they
(19) _____ (write) with pictures on a kind of paper. The name of the Aztec people at the time
(20) _____ (is) 'the Mexica'.

Do you remember?

1 What ___were___ you doing at six o'clock yesterday?
2 I was _____ TV.
3 When I go camping, I sleep in a _____ in my tent.
4 Marco Polo travelled _____ from China to Italy.
5 The teacher was talking _____ the door opened.
6 The street joins the Pyramid of the _____ and the Pyramid of the Moon.

Can do

I can use the past continuous tense to talk about the past.

I can talk about the countryside and follow directions.

I can write directions to places in the countryside.

What can we see in our world?

1 **Read and complete with the correct form of the verbs.**

Marcus Rashford

Marcus Rashford is a famous English footballer. I admire him because he's a great player, but also because he likes (1) _____helping_____ (help) others.

Marcus was born in Manchester on 31st October 1997. As a child, he loved (2) _____ (play) football. The Manchester United schoolboys club chose him as their youngest player ever when he was 11 years old. It was a challenge because he played with older boys, but he achieved great success.

I think Marcus is a good person because he likes (3) _____ (use) his position as a famous footballer to help children in need. He's achieved so much on and off the football field, and he'd like (4) _____ (write) a book because he'd like (5) _____ (help) children to read.

I'd like (6) _____ (achieve) something like Marcus one day because he's a great person. I think it's important to be a role model for young people.

2 **Plan to write a profile. Complete the table for a person you admire.**

Who is it?	_____ is a/an _____ .
Why do you admire him/her?	I admire him/her because _____ .
Where was he/she born, and when?	He/She was born in _____ on _____ .
What did he/she do at school?	At school, he/she _____ .
What was challenging for him/her?	_____ was a challenge, but _____ .
What do you think about his/her achievement?	I think _____ .
What is he/she doing now?	He/She still _____ .
What would you like to achieve one day?	I'd like/love to _____ .

3 📝 **Use your notes to write your profile.**

4 **Did you ...**
- ☐ plan your profile?
- ☐ write about the person's achievements?
- ☐ describe what they like doing and would like to do?
- ☐ read your profile again?
- ☐ check grammar, spelling and punctuation?

Writing tip

Writing a profile
Give lots of different information about a person to make it interesting. You can say the place and the year they were born, what they like to do, and what they would like to do in the future.

1 🎧 13 **Listen and write. There is one example.**

The holiday camp

	Name of camp:	The Lake Camp
1	Price:	_____ pounds a night
2	When:	_____ to 10th October
3	Name of lake:	_____
4	Take:	_____
5	Camp phone number:	_____

4 Food, glorious food!

Countable nouns	Uncountable nouns
We can count them: strawberries, olives …	We can't count them: water, bread …
There **aren't enough** chairs.	There **isn't enough** water.
There **are too many** people.	There**'s too much** bread.

1 Follow the uncountable food words.

How much?

breakfast	pear	strawberry	chips	egg	fries	lunch	lime
orange	burger	fruit juice	chocolate	lemonade	soup	lemon	butter
bread	carrot	flour	sandwich	mango	pasta	sausage	water
rice	milk	meat	coconut	grape	tea	pea	cheese
vegetable	picnic	olives	dinner	beans	coffee	sugar	salt

→ Only a little.

2 Read and match.

1 In some countries there isn't
2 They couldn't make any bread
3 He didn't have many eggs
4 We didn't feel well
5 They had too many strawberries
6 She didn't eat much at lunchtime

a because she felt ill.
b enough food for everyone to eat.
c because they didn't have enough flour.
d so they decided to give some to their friends.
e so he bought some more at the supermarket.
f because we ate too much ice cream at the party.

[ ]
[1]
[ ]
[ ]
[ ]
[ ]

3 Read and choose the right words.

1 I feel ill because I ate **too many** / (**too much**) chocolate this morning.
2 I can't buy that because I haven't got **enough** / **too many** money.
3 Are there **too many** / **too much** sandwiches?
4 There aren't **enough** / **too much** buses in my town.
5 I like going to the beach when there aren't **too much** / **too many** people.
6 There isn't **enough** / **too much** juice for everyone.

4 Write four sentences about your city in your notebook.

There are too many cars.
There aren't enough parks.

Do the online activities on Practice Extra as you complete this unit.

1 Complete the sentences.

aren't enough haven't
is too many too much

1 There __aren't__ enough sandwiches for us.

2 There are _____ people on this bus.

3 Have you got _____ time to help me with the cake, Peter?

4 Oh no! I _____ got enough money!

5 There _____ enough milk for everyone.

6 I think we've got _____ homework this weekend.

2 Complete the conversation. Write a letter (A–F) for each answer.

> A OK. We won't have sausages. I know. Let's have some rice and chicken.
> B Let me see … No, I'm sorry. We haven't got enough spaghetti.
> C That's a good idea. So it's chicken, rice and a salad.
> D Yes, we all like pizza, but there isn't enough flour or enough cheese.
> E I don't know. What would you like?
> F How about some sausages and a salad?

1 What are we going to have for lunch, Dad? [E]

2 Can we have spaghetti, please? It's my favourite. ☐

3 What about pizza then? Can you make us a pizza, please? ☐

4 OK Dad, what ideas have you got? ☐

5 Er, no thanks. I've had too many sausages this week. I had some on Monday and yesterday. ☐

6 That sounds better. Can we have a salad too, please? ☐

3 Write about the picture. Use 'too much', 'too many', 'enough' and the words in the box.

banana cake chair
fork pasta plate water

There are enough chairs. _____
_____
_____
_____
_____
_____

4 What do you think? Answer the questions.

1 Do you eat enough fruit?
_____

2 Do you eat enough fish?
_____

3 Do you eat too much sugar?
_____

4 Do you eat too many sweets?
_____

5 Do you eat too many chips?
_____

6 Do you drink enough water?
_____

1 Label the photos.

biscuit   butter   chopsticks   jam   pan   popcorn   sauce   ~~snack~~

1
snack

2 _____

3 _____

4 _____

5 _____

6 _____

7 _____

8 _____

2 Write the words.

1 We put this on food to make it taste better.
It can be hot or cold. _____sauce_____

2 This is something we eat between meals.
_____

3 These pieces of wood or plastic are used
for eating. _____

4 This is made from fruit. We can put it on
bread. _____

5 We use this to cook in. _____

6 Lots of children like these snacks. They
are often round. _____

7 This snack is popular when people go to
the cinema. _____

8 You can put this on the bread first when
you make sandwiches. _____

3 Write definitions for these words.

1 cereal _____

_____

2 strawberry _____

_____

3 sushi _____

_____

4 Read and complete the sentences with 1, 2, 3 or 4 words.

Potato crisps are very popular as a snack
all over the world. George Crum invented
them in the USA. At the restaurant where
he worked, fries were popular. One day
someone wasn't pleased because the
fries were too thick. Crum made them
thinner and thinner until finally, he made
fries that were too thin to eat with a fork.
The man in the restaurant was happy
and people around the world started
to eat potato crisps. In the USA, crisps
are called 'chips' and in the UK, fries are
called 'chips'.

1 Potato crisps are a __very popular__
snack all over the world.

2 A man from _____ invented
them.

3 He made the first crisps because a man
thought his fries _____.

4 Finally, Crum made fries that were
_____ with a fork.

5 Fries are called 'chips' in _____.

1 Match the children to their snacks. Write sentences.

Helen   Tanaz   Michael

Kito   Akash   Robert

1 Helen's favourite snack is bread and butter.
2 _____
3 _____
4 _____
5 _____
6 _____

2 Read the poem. Find the word.

The first letter in 'snack'. I'm hungry, you see. [s]

The second in 'jam'. The fruit's from a tree. [ ]

The third in 'sausage'. A hot dog to eat. [ ]

The fourth in 'popcorn'. Salted or sweet. [ ]

The fifth in 'butter'. I love it on bread. [ ]

It's something to do with food, I said.

Look at the word and write the letter.

With me, for sure, a dish will taste better.

What am I? _____

3 Read and answer 'yes' or 'no'.

Chopsticks

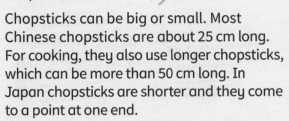

People in Asia use many different things to eat with, for example hands, spoons, forks, knives and chopsticks.

Chopsticks can be big or small. Most Chinese chopsticks are about 25 cm long. For cooking, they also use longer chopsticks, which can be more than 50 cm long. In Japan chopsticks are shorter and they come to a point at one end.

Chopsticks are made of a number of materials, but most are made of wood or plastic. A long time ago they put silver on the end of the chopsticks.

Things you should or shouldn't do when you eat with chopsticks

- Do not move your chopsticks around.
- Do not pick food up by making a hole in it with your chopsticks.
- Do not pull dishes towards you with chopsticks. Use your hands.
- Pull dishes close to you when eating. Put them back after you use them.
- You can lift your dish up to your mouth to eat small pieces of food.

1 Chopsticks are always 25 cm long.
   no
2 They are the same size in Japan and China. _____
3 They are usually made of plastic or wood. _____
4 You should use them to make holes. _____
5 You should use them to pull dishes towards you. _____
6 You should use them to pick up your food. _____

Vocabulary: food   39

Sounds and life skills
Exploring food from other cultures
Pronunciation focus

1 🎧 14 **Listen and circle the strong words.**

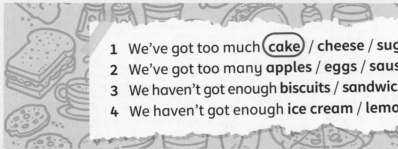

1 We've got too much (cake) / cheese / sugar!
2 We've got too many **apples** / eggs / sausages!
3 We haven't got enough **biscuits** / sandwiches / watermelon!
4 We haven't got enough **ice cream** / lemonade / water!

2 🎧 15 **Read and complete with your own words. Listen and say.**

We're having a picnic, but we've got too many _____ and too much
_____ , but we haven't got any _____ ! What are we going to do?

3 **Read and complete.**

apples   bread   Empanadas   India   ~~rice~~   Sashimi

What do you know about world food?

1 You will find a lot of _____ rice _____ in Spanish paella.

2 Tandoori chicken comes from _____ .

3 _____ is made of raw fish and comes from Japan.

4 _____ are tasty pastries, usually with meat inside.

5 You need _____ to make tarte Tatin.

6 Simit is a Turkish _____ in the shape of a circle.

4 **Read and complete.**

My favourite food is _____ .
I like food from _____ .
I've never eaten _____ .
Today, I've eaten _____ .
I sometimes eat too many _____ .
I don't eat enough _____ .

1 Read and answer.

Diggory Bones

1 Why will Diggory have to work quickly? <u>They've only got enough food for three days.</u>
2 When will Iyam tell Diggory where the Sun Stone is? _____
3 Where are the secret caves? _____
4 Why was corn important to the Mayas and the Aztecs? _____
5 What did the Aztecs eat with chocolate? _____
6 What other food did the Aztecs eat? _____

2 Correct the sentences.

1 Emily didn't ask Iyam enough questions.
<u>Emily asked Iyam too many questions.</u>
2 There are pictures of sushi on the Sun Stone.
_____
3 Butter was the most important Aztec food.
_____
4 The door to the caves is about three kilometres west.
_____
5 Iyam shouldn't run because the ground is moving.
_____
6 Diggory asked Emily to get him some chopsticks.
_____

Do you remember?

1 We've got too ____many____ strawberries.
2 We haven't got _____ milk.
3 I love butter and strawberry _____ on my bread in the morning.
4 People in China often use _____ to eat with.
5 _____ is a Spanish rice dish.
6 We cook _____ in a pan of boiling water.

Can do

I can use countable and uncountable nouns.

I can talk about food.

I can write about my favourite food.

How does food get to your table?

1 Read and complete with the correct form of the verbs.

> grow   make   plant   prepares   take   wash

Potatoes: from field to fork

1 Potatoes _____grow_____ from spring to autumn.
2 First, a large machine _____ the fields for potato planting.
3 Then farmers _____ potato seeds about 15 cm underground.
4 A large machine collects the potatoes when they're ready. Next, lorries _____ the potatoes to a factory.
5 After that, factory workers _____ and then sort the potatoes into different sizes.
6 Finally, we can eat the potatoes! We often _____ them into chips and crisps.

2 Plan to write a presentation. Complete the table about a food or drink.

What is the food or drink?	_____
Where/When does it grow?	It grows / They grow in/on _____.
When is the harvest?	_____
How does it get to your table?	First, _____. Then _____ Next, _____. After that, _____. Finally, _____.
How can people eat or drink it?	_____

3 Use your notes to write your presentation.

4 Did you ...

- ☐ plan your presentation?
- ☐ use sequencing words?
- ☐ use the correct words to show each step of the process?
- ☐ read your presentation again?
- ☐ check grammar, spelling and punctuation?

Writing tip

Writing a presentation
Use sequencing words like **first, then, next, after that** and **finally** to make your presentation easy for other people to understand.

Biology: potatoes | 🛡 critical thinking

Flyers Reading and Writing Part 7

1 **Look at the three pictures. Write about this story. Write 20 or more words.**

_____

_____

_____

_____

1 **Read the story. Choose a word from the box. Write the correct word next to numbers 1–8.**

> camp   camping   chopsticks   ~~countryside~~   enough   hungry
> map   pasta   rucksack   sandwiches   tents   too   torch   was   were

FRIENDLY

Last week's episode of **Friendly** was really funny because there was a school trip to the ___countryside___ . The teachers were taking their pupils to a forest to (1) _____ . On Friday afternoon when they were waiting for the bus outside the school, Jenny arrived with a really big, heavy suitcase. She said that her (2) _____ wasn't very big and she had lots of equipment.

On the way to the campsite Sally sat next to the bus driver because she wanted to watch her drive, look at the directions and follow them on her (3) _____ .

When they got to the forest, all five of them had to help Jenny to pull her suitcase across the field to the (4) _____ . The ground was too soft and it was really hard work. When they were pulling the suitcase, it fell over again and again.

It was dinner time when they arrived at the campsite, and they were dirty, tired and (5) _____ . Jenny wasn't very pleased when she discovered she couldn't use her hairdryer. She was surprised because she couldn't connect it to any electricity in the wall of the tent! Peter was really unhappy because he wanted to cook sausages and beans, but Jim thought a fire was (6) _____ dangerous in a forest. Jim took some peanut butter and jam (7) _____ out of his rucksack, Sally said she had some popcorn and biscuits, and they all laughed when Frankie said she was carrying enough cold sushi and (8) _____ for everyone! They all agreed that they were eating the strangest camp menu ever!

2 **Now choose the best name for the story.**

Tick one box.   A drive in the country ☐   An unusual dinner ☐   Forest fire ☐

3 **Which is the odd one out and why?**

1 soup   butter   jam   (biscuit)
  It's countable.

2 chopsticks   fork   torch   spoon
  _____

3 best   north   east   south
  _____

4 sandwich   sauce   pan   snack
  _____

5 tent   cave   sleeping bag   rucksack
  _____

6 pasta   bread   cake   cheese
  _____

4 Complete the sentences. Count and write the letters.

1 The opposite of east is ___west___ . [4]

2 We put _____ with peanut butter in sandwiches. [ ]

3 They travelled from Italy to China. It was a long _____ . [ ]

4 A _____ is like a small house. We sleep in it when we camp. [ ]

5 A _____ is higher than a hill. [ ]

6 They use _____ to eat sushi in Japan. [ ]

7 We use a _____ to see in the dark when we go camping. [ ]

8 I don't like this soup. There's _____ much salt in it. [ ]

9 Go from one place to another.
_____ [ ]

10 How _____ butter do we need? [ ]

11 A bag which we carry on our back is a _____ . [ ]

12 There were too _____ people at the beach. [ ]

13 'What _____ he doing when he fell?' 'He was skiing.' [ ]

14 Something light which we eat between meals when we're hungry is a _____ . [ ]

15 We only had 50 g of flour. It wasn't _____ flour to make biscuits. [ ]

5 Now complete the crossword. Write the message.

3
8
2
6   9
5
w
e
1   4   s
10
t
7

1 2 3 4 5 6 7   8 9 10
[ ][ ][ ][ ][ ][ ][ ] [ ][ ][t] !

6 Quiz time!

1 When did Lenny break his arm?
When he was

2 What pushes together to make a mountain range?
_____

3 What's the world's oldest mountain range? _____

4 Why couldn't Stella, Lenny and Meera make the cake?
_____

5 What climate do apples need to grow?
_____

6 How many different types of apples are there around the world?
_____

7 Write questions for your quiz in your notebook.

STUDY AGAIN | Present perfect and adverbs

We **still** haven't chosen a project. (= But we have to do it soon.)
The rescue people have been here **since** ten o'clock. (= When? A point in time: time, date, day, etc.)
It's been here **for** about three hours. (= How long? How many minutes, hours, days, weeks, etc.)

1 **Read and choose the right words.**

1 Mr Schwarz has taught me German **for** / **since** / **still** three years.

2 It hasn't snowed since **three days** / **Saturday** / **two weeks.**

3 I **still** / **for** / **since** haven't finished this activity.

4 They **are** / **have** / **were** worked here for a year.

5 She hasn't caught a fish **for** / **since** / **still** two hours.

2 **Complete the sentences with 'for' or 'since'.**

1 She's lived in her village ___since___ 2008.

2 My little brother has studied English _____ six months.

3 I haven't seen Deniz _____ Monday.

4 Mum's had her favourite jacket _____ ten years!

5 I haven't eaten anything _____ nine o'clock.

3 **Look at the code (a = ____). Write the secret message.**

a	b	c
d	e	f
g	h	i

j	k	l
m	n	o
p	q	r

s	t	u
v	w	x
y	z	

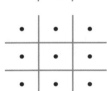
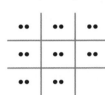

I ' v e

4 📝 **Write a message in code in your notebook.**

🔼 Do the online activities on **Practice Extra** as you complete this unit

1 **Find and write four sentences.**

liked fishing	three o'clock.	this lesson since
in that flat for	five years.	We've been in
~~He's loved~~	I've	for nine months.
started school.	They've lived	~~maths since he~~

He's loved maths since he _____

_____

_____

 2 **Write sentences about you with 'for' or 'since'.**

1 (this room)   I've been in this room for ten minutes.

2 (this class)   _____

3 (best friend)   _____

4 (this school)   _____

5 (my house)   _____

6 (English)   _____

 3 **Use the ideas in Activity 2 to write questions to ask your partner.**

1   How long have you been in this room?

2   _____

3   _____

4   _____

5   _____

6   _____

4 **Read and complete the table.**

It's 12 o'clock. There are four children on a bus. Peter was the first boy on the bus. He's been on the bus for ten minutes now, but he's going to get off at the next stop, in two minutes.

David was the last to get on. He got on two minutes ago, but he's going to get off last.

Anika has been on the bus for four minutes. She's going to get off at the same stop as Emma.

Emma has been on the bus for the same time as Anika. She's going to get off at the stop after Peter, in four minutes' time.

Anika and Emma are going to get off the bus seven minutes before David.

	Got on the bus?	Going to get off the bus?	How long on the bus in total?
Peter	11.50		
David			
Anika			
Emma			

Language: present perfect with *for, since, still*   47

1 Look and complete the crossword.

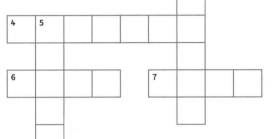
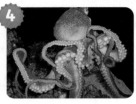

¹j e l ²l y f i ³s h

4 5

6   7

2 Write the words.

1 Big ones have got the biggest eyes in the world. ___squid___

2 It's got eight legs, but it hasn't got a shell. _____

3 It has no brain or bones but it eats tiny fish and animals. _____

4 The salt water which covers Earth. _____

5 It's got eight legs, two claws and a hard shell. It walks from side to side. _____

6 It's a mammal which lives in the sea. It isn't a dolphin or a whale. _____

7 It's a sea animal that forms reefs. _____

8 It's a sea animal with big claws and a hard shell. _____

3 Read, look and write the words.

(1) ___Fishing___ is a very important activity. Every year people eat more than 100 million tonnes

of (2) _____ (one tonne is a thousand kilos). That's a lot of fish, so we need to be careful and

not catch too many.

People don't only eat fish though. In different countries people eat lots of other sea creatures.

Inuit people eat (3) _____ . In Japan and Greece (4) _____ and

(5) _____ are favourite foods, and (6) _____ are popular all over the world.

In some countries, the USA and France for example, people pay a lot of (7) _____ to eat

(8) _____ .

Circle 12 words. Which two are different? Why?

beautiful (loud) angeroustrongreaturtlexcitedolphinicexcitingoodirty

_____ and _____ are different. They are _____ .

 Compare these sea animals. Use adjectives from Activity 1 and your own ideas.

1 jellyfish – seals _Jellyfish are more dangerous than seals._____
2 coral – an octopus _____
3 an octopus – a jellyfish _____
4 turtles – lobsters _____
5 a whale – a squid _____
6 a shark – a crab _____

3 **Read and colour and write.**

Find the octopus which is sitting on the big rock and colour it purple. Next, find the squid (there are three), and colour the smallest one yellow. At the bottom of the picture there's a lot of coral. Colour it red. Have you found the lobster? It's in the bottom right corner. Write 'lobster' above it. At the top of the picture there are some jellyfish. Colour the biggest one blue. Finally, there's only one more animal to colour. Find the crab (there are three), and colour the one inside the big shell pink.

 Read and match.

1 The world's first coral reef
2 Storms can
3 Scientists have used coral reefs
4 When parrot fish eat coral,
5 The biggest reef in the world

a is the Great Barrier Reef in Australia.
b appeared about 500 million years ago. [1]
c they make beautiful white sand.
d to make a lot of different medicines.
e break coral reefs.

Sounds and life skills
Finding out more
Pronunciation focus

1 🎧 16 **Listen and circle the correct word.**

1 The (people) / team pulled the **dolphin** / **boat** back to the **beach** / **park**.

2 My **mother** / **sister** and **father** / **brother** like to eat **breakfast** / **dinner** together.

3 A **dolphin** / **penguin** can swim in different kinds of **water** / **weather**.

4 Look over **here** / **there**! My brother's bought a **blue** / **purple** and red **bike** / **parrot**.

2 🎧 17 **Complete with the words from Activity 1. Listen and check.**

/p/	/b/	/d/	/ ð/
			mother

3 **Read and write the questions.**

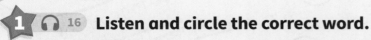

a / fire? / there / Is

A: What's happening? ⁽¹⁾ Is there a fire?

B: No, the fire fighters are rescuing a cat.

the / at / cat / the / moment? / Where's

A: ⁽²⁾ _____

B: Look! It's up there in that tree.

time? / Has / been / there / a / it / long

A: ⁽³⁾ _____

B: It's been there since eight o'clock this morning.

fire fighters / What / the / done? / have

A: ⁽⁴⁾ _____

B: They've put up a ladder.

they / to / do? / going / What / are

A: ⁽⁵⁾ _____

B: They are going to climb the ladder and bring the cat down.

4 **Read and complete.**   arrived   called   climbed   had   ~~rescued~~   is   was

This afternoon, fire fighters ⁽¹⁾ ___rescued___ Tilly the cat from a very tall tree in Pine Grove Road. Tilly ⁽²⁾ _____ in the tree for a long time. The family ⁽³⁾ _____ the fire fighters and they ⁽⁴⁾ _____ at 12 o'clock. They put up a ladder and ⁽⁵⁾ _____ the tree. Tilly the cat ⁽⁶⁾ _____ now safe at home with her family. What an adventure she's ⁽⁷⁾ _____ !

1 Read and answer.

1 What has Emily found? <u>She's found a torch.</u>
2 What did Quetzalcoatl get at Teotihuacan? _____
3 What kind of shell has Diggory seen? _____
4 Why's Iyam like this animal? _____
5 Was gold a treasure for the Aztecs? _____
6 What's Richard going to do if they don't help Iyam? _____

2 Write sentences from the story.

1 You / pull / these plants / you / open / this cave
<u>You've pulled these plants and you've opened this cave.</u>
2 I / find / torch
_____
3 I / know / about / these caves / 1971
_____
4 This / be / place / their gods / make / Sun / Moon / universe
_____
5 There / be / gold here / hundreds of years
_____
6 Richard / use / my mobile / follow us
_____

Do you remember?

1 I've been here ____since____ seven o'clock.
2 She's lived in this town _____ five years.
3 _____ have been in our seas and oceans for 650 million years.
4 I think _____ reefs are really beautiful.
5 Giant squids have the _____ eyes in the world.
6 Seals have swum in our seas for 22 million _____ .

Can do

I can talk about things that have happened using **for** and **since**.
I can talk about sea animals.
I can write about sea animals.

How can we make electricity?

1 **Read and complete.**

> Another reason is that   Firstly, it's a   On the other hand, a disadvantage of
> ~~There are lots of advantages of~~   To sum up, I think that

Study Guide Page 12

Geothermal Energy

Inside our planet, it's very hot. Geothermal energy uses the heat from the Earth to make electricity. The heat is under the ground, and special buildings called power plants change the heat into electricity. (1) _There are lots of advantages of_ geothermal energy. (2) _____ renewable source of energy so it's clean for the environment. (3) _____ it's a good way to create electricity in areas where there are volcanoes, like in Iceland. (4) _____ geothermal energy is that the power plants are very expensive to build. (5) _____ geothermal energy, like solar, wind and wave, is a really good source of renewable energy.

2 **Plan to write an essay. Complete the table on a source of renewable energy.**

Introduction	_____ is a type of renewable energy, which means it uses _____ .
Advantages	There are lots of reasons why people think _____ is a good idea. Firstly, _____ . Another reason is that _____ . Finally, _____ .
Disadvantages	On the other hand, a disadvantage of _____ is that _____ .
Ending	To sum up, I believe that _____ .

3 📝 **Use your notes to write your essay.**

4 **Did you ...**
- ☐ plan your essay?
- ☐ include an introduction and an ending?
- ☐ use topic sentences?
- ☐ read your essay again?
- ☐ check grammar, spelling and punctuation?

Writing tip

Writing an essay
You can organise the information in your essay with an **introduction**, some **advantages**, some **disadvantages**, and an **ending**. Topic sentences help to introduce a new idea in each part of your essay.

1 **Sarah is talking to her friend. What does Katy say to Sarah?**

Read the conversation and choose the best answer.
Write a letter (A–E) for each answer.
There is one example.

Example

Sarah:	Hi Katy! I haven't seen you for a long time.
Katy:	C

Questions

1 **Sarah:** That's nice. Did you go anywhere interesting?
    Katy: _____

2 **Sarah:** Oh! I haven't been there. Did you like it?
    Katy: _____

3 **Sarah:** I'll ask my mum to take me next week.
    Katy: _____

4 **Sarah:** Which is the best day to go, do you think?
    Katy: _____

A   Yes, it was great. There were lots of things to do.

B   Friday. That's when you can swim with the dolphins.

C   I know. I've been on holiday. **(Example)**

D   Yes. I went to the 'Sea Life' centre.

E   That's a good idea.

6 Free time

some	any	no	every
someone	**any**one	**no** one	**every**one
something	**any**thing	**no**thing	**every**thing
somewhere	**any**where	**no**where	**every**where

1 Read the test carefully. Follow the instructions.

Reading Test

1 First read ALL the instructions.

2 Write the name of someone you like.
_____

3 Think of somewhere you like going.
_____

4 Name something you can use to write.
_____

5 Write your full name.
_____

6 Write somewhere you can sleep.
_____

7 Only write the answers to numbers 5 and 8.
_____

8 Name someone who teaches you.
_____

2 Read and choose the right words.

1 I can't see **anything** / **something**.
2 Is there **everywhere** / **anywhere** I can sit down?
3 I couldn't find my book and I looked **everywhere** / **somewhere**.
4 Can **no one** / **anyone** give me a pencil, please?
5 Have you got **nothing** / **anything** made of plastic?
6 **Everyone** / **Anyone** stand up, please.

3 Read and complete.

> anyone   everywhere
> everywhere   inside
> ~~no one~~   no one

A man is watching TV when he hears the doorbell. He opens it but ⁽¹⁾ ___no one___ is there. He looks ⁽²⁾ _____ : to the left, to the right, up and finally he looks down and he sees a snail. He's angry and he closes the door quickly. He then goes back ⁽³⁾ _____ his house.

A month later, the same thing happens. He opens the door but there isn't ⁽⁴⁾ _____ there. He looks ⁽⁵⁾ _____ , but there's ⁽⁶⁾ _____ there. Finally, he looks down and sees the snail again. Before he can close the door quickly again, the snail says, 'Why did you do that?'

4 Tell the story in the past. Write it in your notebook.

Read and answer.

1 In this sport everyone wears boots. There are 11 players in a team and anyone can kick something which is round. Not everyone can catch the round thing. Only one player can do that.
  a What's the thing which they kick?
  ___a ball___
  b What's the sport? _____
  c Who are the people who play this sport?

  _____

2 In this sport someone puts some long things on their feet and goes to the top of a hill or a mountain. They go down the hill over something which is cold and white.
  a What are the long things which they put on their feet? _____
  b What are they doing? _____
  c What's the thing which is cold and white? _____

3 In this sport everyone uses something long to hit something which is very small and round. No one can kick, catch or throw the small, round thing. They have to hit it into a small hole.
  a What's the sport? _____
  b Do you play it inside or outside?

  _____
  c Where is the hole? _____

 Write a definition for a sport or a hobby. Use the words from the 'Study again' box on page 54.

_____
_____
_____
_____
_____
_____

 Match the sentences with the pictures.

> a Would anyone like to play tennis?
> b Let's go somewhere different on holiday this year.
> c No one wants to play soccer today.
> d There's nowhere for us to play.

Read and order the text.

☐ but No one did it. Someone was angry, because really it was something that Everyone

☐ In the end Everyone was really angry with Someone when No one did what Anyone could do.

[1] Once upon a time there were four children in a class. Their names

☐ classroom. Everyone thought that Someone was going to do it. It wasn't difficult, so Anyone could do it,

☐ could do. Everyone thought that Anyone could do it, but No one thought that Everyone wasn't going to do it.

☐ were No one, Anyone, Someone and Everyone. Their teacher asked for some help in the

1 Label the photos.

   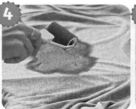 

1 b e a t b o x   3 _ _ _ _ _ _ _ _ _   5 _ _ _ _ _ _ _ _ _ _ _ _ _

2 _ _ _ _ _ _   4 _ _ _ _ _ _ _ _ _ _ _

2 Follow the free time words.

hobby	does	ballet dancing	sewing	playing the piano	baseball
clothes design	to	beatbox	Someone	different	chess
skateboarding	places	table tennis	bored.	goes	skating
mountain biking	things	cooking	interesting	never	reading
board games	skiing	golf	and	is	who

3 Look at the other words in Activity 2. Use them to write a sentence.

Someone _____

_____

4 Read and answer.

When people first started free running, they did it to get from one place to another using the quickest path. They ran and jumped from wall to wall, and down steps. Now they try to do it in the most beautiful way possible. Free running is similar to Parkour.

In Britain, free running became popular in 2003 after someone made a TV programme about it.

Free running has also been in music videos by pop stars, and we can see it in action films and adverts on TV. There is also a **Free running** video game.

It is important to remember that it is something which not everyone can do because free runners need to be very strong and fit. It is also difficult and it can be dangerous.

1 What do free runners do? They run and jump from wall to wall and down steps.

2 When did free running become popular in Britain? _____

3 Where can you see free running? _____

4 Can everyone do free running? _____

5 Why / Why not? _____

1 Find and say four differences. Then write sentences.

In picture a, a girl and a boy are playing chess. In picture b, two girls are playing.

_____

_____

_____

2 Read the email. Choose the right words and write them on the lines.

Hi Betty,

How are you? Did (1) ____you____ have a good holiday? (2) _____ was great. I went to a special activity camp and I've started some new hobbies. (3) _____ was at the camp for five days and (4) _____ did something different every day! The first two days it was raining so we did puzzles, played board games and I learned to play chess. I also designed some clothes!

On Wednesday they took (5) _____ to the hills where we rode amazing mountain bikes. It was really exciting. William taught (6) _____ how to skateboard on Thursday morning so I spent all afternoon skateboarding with my friends. Friday was (7) _____ last day and we did beatbox and rap!

(8) _____ only problem now is that I have too many hobbies!

Holly

1	they	you	us
2	Mine	I	You
3	He	We	I
4	him	we	them
5	we	they	us
6	me	her	you
7	his	me	our
8	I	Me	My

3 Write questions for the answers.

1 <u>Where did she go?</u>
She went to an activity camp.

2 _____
She was there for five days.

3 _____
Because it was raining.

4 _____
She learned to play chess.

5 _____
They rode amazing mountain bikes.

6 _____
They did beatbox and rap.

4 Write an email to a friend about your hobbies in your notebook.

Vocabulary: hobbies   57

Sounds and life skills
Imagining and inventing
Pronunciation focus

1 🎧 18 **Listen and draw arrows ↘↗.**

Joe: I'm bored! Dad, can I use yesterday's newspaper, please?
Dad: Yes, of course.
Hannah: Mum, can I have that old plant pot, please?
Mum: Yes. Here you are.

2 **Write questions asking a friend for different things. Then draw arrows ↘↗.**

Ebony, can I borrow your bike tomorrow, please?

1 _____

2 _____

3 _____

3 **Read and complete. Then look and match.**   boots   bottles   paper   shells   ~~sock~~

1	2	3	4	5
c	☐	☐	☐	☐

a Collect _____ on the beach and make this wind instrument.

b Paint old glass and plastic _____ and make a chess game!

c You can use a ____sock____ to make a puppet.

d Recycle _____ and make planes for a flying competition.

e Use these _____ for your plants!

4 **Explain how you can reuse an object. Draw a picture to help you.**

Use a _____

_____

_____

_____

1 Read and answer.

Diggory Bones

1 Where are they going to go? <u>Somewhere nearer the sea.</u>
2 What will take Iyam to a cave of gold? _____
3 Are Kukulcan and Quetzalcoatl the same?
   _____
4 What's Kukulcan's temple called?
   _____
5 What did the Mayas do before their ball game?
   _____
6 In which months can you see the snake on the stairs?
   _____

A Mayan ball court

2 📝 Look at the code. Write the secret message in your notebook.

N = north
E = east
S = south
W = west

Tlachtli – 5E – 4S – 2W – 3N – 3W – 3S – 4E – 4N – 1S – 3W – 3S – 2N – 4E – 2W –
2N – 1W – 4S – 1N – 2W – 5E – 2N – 3W – 1S – 2W – 4E – 1S – 1W – 2W – 3N.

Tlachtli	walls.	ball	rubber	played.	was
which	had	stone	game	They	of
up	pass	high	heavy	in	a
circle	the	a	of	one	made
Mayan	to	through	ball	men	a

Do you remember?

1 Is there ___anywhere___ I can sit down?
2 I've looked _____ but I can't find my pen.
3 _____ is a very old board game.
4 Music and rhythm which you make with your mouth is called _____.
5 I enjoy riding on the bike _____ in the mountains.
6 My friend is (act) _____ in a play this weekend.

Can do

I can use **something, anything, nothing** and **everything**.
I can talk about different hobbies.
I can write about sports and activities.

What makes a funfair ride exciting and safe?

1 **Read and complete.**

different   fantastic   ~~new~~   scarier   strange   under

A Day at the Funfair

Last weekend, I went to a funfair with my friends because we wanted to try a (1) ___new___ rollercoaster ride called Upside Down.

It was (2) _____ from all of the other rollercoaster rides which I've been on because on this rollercoaster you ride (3) _____ the tracks! We sat in seats with our legs hanging free, which felt very (4) _____ at first. Of course, we wore a harness too.

I thought the ride was (5) _____ than other rollercoaster rides because there were twists and turns, and we went around five different loops. It was (6) _____! I want to go back to the funfair again soon just to ride on Upside Down.

2 **Plan to write a story. Complete the table about a funfair ride.**

Paragraph 1	When was it? Where were you? Who were you with?	
Paragraph 2	What happened? How did you feel?	
Paragraph 3	What happened in the end? How did you feel?	

3 📝 **Use your notes to write your story.**

4 **Did you ...**
- [ ] plan your story?
- [ ] include a beginning, middle and ending?
- [ ] use interesting adjectives to tell your story?
- [ ] read your story again?
- [ ] check grammar, spelling and punctuation?

Writing tip

Writing a story

When you write a story about something that has already happened, you can use **past verbs** and lots of different **adjectives** to make your story interesting.

I **went** to a big funfair with my friends last week. It **was** really **exciting** because ...

Design: rollercoasters | 🛡 creative thinking

1 **Read the story. Choose a word from the box. Write the correct word next to numbers 1–5. There is one example.**

example				
help	them	playing	basement	space
often	plays	want	parents	countryside

Rachel and Paul ____help____ at an animal rescue centre in their free time. They **(1)** _____ go there at the weekend. They love **(2)** _____ with the dogs and cats. They also help to look after **(3)** _____ . They feed the animals and clean their boxes. They really enjoy doing this because they love animals.

They sometimes go to a special market with their **(4)** _____ and other grown-ups. At the market they sell things to get money for the rescue centre. They also ask other people to help them. One day a rich and famous actor went to the rescue centre and took two big dogs and three cats home to his house in the **(5)** _____ . He lives in a castle!

(6) **Now choose the best name for the story.**

Tick one box.

Friends and family ☐

Pet rescue ☐

A day at the market ☐

Review Units 5 and 6

1 **Read the story. Choose a word from the box. Write the correct word next to numbers 1–8.**

anything   chess   cook   coral reef   dangerous   everyone   ~~hobbies~~
holiday   no one   nowhere   ocean   ridden   safe   someone   squid

FRIENDLY

In today's episode, the friends are talking about the
_____hobbies_____ that they do in their free time. Jim's started
free running and is really excited about it. He says he
got the idea when he saw the film **Captain America: The
Winter Soldier** and the hero had to run through a city
centre. Sally says she loves action films and that there
are special actors who do all the tricks. Her favourite
is Maxine Limit. Maxine has driven cars at over 200
kilometres an hour, she's flown lots of different planes and she's (1) _____ motorbikes,
horses and elephants. Jenny doesn't find any of this exciting and she tells Jim that she thinks his
new hobby is strange and too (2) _____ .
Frankie's hobby isn't dangerous, but once when she was painting a small waterfall in the
countryside, she fell into the river, which was moving very fast, and (3) _____ had to pull
her out. Peter loves trying new things to eat. He says he'll try anything. He's eaten octopus and
(4) _____ before, but on his last (5) _____ in Japan, he and his parents ate
blowfish. This fish is very, very poisonous and someone has to prepare and (6) _____ it
very well or you can die when you eat it. Jenny tries to remember the most dangerous thing she's
ever done. Jim laughs because he can't believe she's ever done (7) _____ dangerous.
Jenny says that once she ate one of Frankie's dishes and (8) _____ knows that she's a
terrible cook!

2 **Now choose the best name for the story.**

Tick one box.   Living dangerously ☐   Hard actors ☐   Eating seafood ☐

3 **Which is the odd one out and why?**

1 golf (badminton) soccer tennis
  You don't play it with a ball.

2 seen   ridden   walked   thought
  _____

3 baseball   volleyball   soccer   basketball
  _____

4 crab   jellyfish   lobster   turtle
  _____

5 skates   skis   chess   skateboards
  _____

6 octopus   jellyfish   seal   clownfish
  _____

4 Complete the sentences. Count and write the letters.

1 'How many fish has that dolphin _____eaten_____ ?' 'Six.' [5]

2 In _____ people run and jump through a city centre. [ ]

3 A sea animal without claws which has got eight legs. It isn't a squid. _____ [ ]

4 _____ is a black and white board game. [ ]

5 An _____ is usually bigger than seas, rivers and lakes. [ ]

6 'Is there _____ in the café?' 'No, everyone's gone.' [ ]

7 A _____ is something hard on the outside of an animal's body. A turtle's got one. [ ]

8 We stand on a _____ to go fast in parks. [ ]

9 A _____ is a round animal with eight legs and two arms with claws. [ ]

10 He's been a footballer _____ 2005. [ ]

11 _____ looks like a little forest but it's lots of sea animals. [ ]

12 A _____ is in the same family as dolphins and seals, but it's much bigger. [ ]

13 A bat is _____ which we use to hit a ball. [ ]

14 'How long have you _____ your mountain bike?' 'A year.' [ ]

15 He's been a photographer _____ nine years. [ ]

5 Now complete the crossword. Write the message.

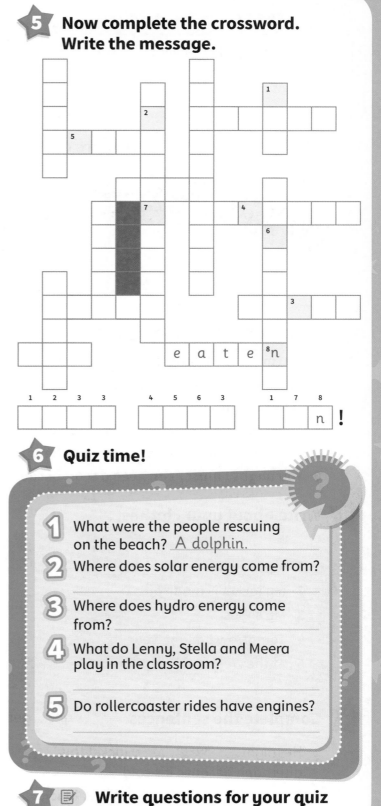

e a t e n !

6 Quiz time!

1 What were the people rescuing on the beach? A dolphin.

2 Where does solar energy come from? _____

3 Where does hydro energy come from? _____

4 What do Lenny, Stella and Meera play in the classroom? _____

5 Do rollercoaster rides have engines? _____

7 📝 Write questions for your quiz in your notebook.

7 Fashion sense

I think it **may look** better with a jacket.	I **might buy** a new jacket.
I **might not need** a jacket.	She **may go** to the party.

1 **Circle 12 words. Which two are different? Why?**

_____ and _____ are different.

They are _____ .

jacket trousers skateboard dress shoe shirt trainers weater unning lasses socks kirt

2 **Read and choose the right words.**

1 He **may buy** / **may buys** / **may to buy** some new trainers.

2 She **mights wear** / **might wears** / **might wear** her gold bracelet.

3 It **not might** / **might not** / **isn't might** be cold.

4 You **may prefer** / **mays prefer** / **may prefers** olives on your pizza.

5 They **can't might** / **might not** / **don't might** win this afternoon's game.

6 You **might** / **must** / **can** need a scarf because I think it's cold outside!

3 **Write about your clothes.**

1 My trainers are made of _____ .

2 My jacket is made of _____ .

3 My shoes _____ .

4 Tomorrow I might wear _____ because _____ .

5 At the weekend I might wear _____ because _____ .

4 **Complete the sentences.** | get   get up   go   visit   watch   ~~wear~~ |

1 He might ___wear___ a jacket this afternoon because it's cold.

2 She might _____ TV after lunch.

3 They might _____ us today.

4 You might not _____ your present until Sunday.

5 I may not _____ shopping tomorrow.

6 We may _____ early on Saturday.

1 What do you think it is? Use 'may'.

It may be _____   _____   _____   _____

_____   _____   _____   _____

2 Look at the picture. Read and answer 'yes' or 'no'.

1 They might have a picnic. __yes__
2 She might be lost. _____
3 He may want to catch a bus home. _____
4 She might not be happy. _____
5 It might rain. _____
6 They might need coats. _____

3 Correct the sentences.

1 They mights wear their jeans. _They might wear their jeans._
2 She does might take a jacket. _____
3 I don't might put on my sweater. _____
4 Lucas may plays football tomorrow. _____
5 I might not to wear my black shoes. _____
6 They mays wear their new trainers. _____

4 Find and write five sentences.

Susan	might put	is green	coats and scarves.
Our school	took	of	and red.
Kito	uniform	on their	plastic.
My schoolbag's	wore her	blue spotted	with him.
The children	made	a jacket	belt.

1 _Susan wore her blue spotted belt._
2 _____
3 _____
4 _____
5 _____

1 **Find two words for each group of letters. One is a clothes word.**

1 tr- <u>trainers</u> , <u>traffic</u>
2 sh- _____ , _____
3 po- _____ , _____
4 gl- _____ , _____
5 u- _____ , _____
6 bu- _____ , _____

mbrella   oves   ~~ainers~~   ue

orts   ~~affic~~   gly

tter

opping   cket

tato   tton

2 **Label the photos with clothes words from Activity 1.**

<u>pocket</u>

3 **Read and complete the sentences with 1, 2, 3 or 4 words.**

Last Saturday Oliver went shopping with his Uncle Harry to buy some new clothes. They went to three different clothes shops. The first shop was called Legs Eleven and they had lots of socks. Oliver chose some grey and green ones.

Next they went to look for some shorts. They found lots in a shop called 4 Fashion. Oliver didn't know which ones to choose, so his uncle helped him. He got a cool orange pair made of cotton, with big pockets.

In the last clothes shop they bought a striped brown and red coat. He didn't buy any new trainers because he's got three pairs at home. When they were coming home, it started to rain so they bought two umbrellas from a small shop. They caught the bus home because they didn't want to get wet.

1 Oliver went to the shops with _____<u>his Uncle Harry</u>_____ .
2 Legs Eleven was _____ shop which they went into.
3 Oliver's new socks are _____ .
4 Uncle Harry helped Oliver _____ some shorts.
5 Oliver's new orange shorts are made of _____ and they have big pockets.
6 He didn't need _____ because he's got three pairs.
7 They got a striped _____ in the last clothes shop.
8 They went home on _____ because it was raining.

1 Read and complete the circle with names and clothes words.

Three girls and two boys are sitting round a table. Frank is sitting between two girls. The girl on his left is called Emma.

The girl on William's left is called Betty.

The girl between Frank and Sarah is wearing a striped T-shirt and a skirt. She has a beautiful gold ring.

The boy with the shorts is wearing a belt. He's also wearing a shirt and a new jacket.

The girl with the scarf isn't wearing a skirt. She's wearing some trousers and a sweater which is made of cotton.

The girl on the right of Frank has got some plastic earrings on. She's also wearing a striped sweater, a skirt and trainers.

The other boy is cold so he's wearing some gloves. His sweater is striped and he's also wearing trousers.

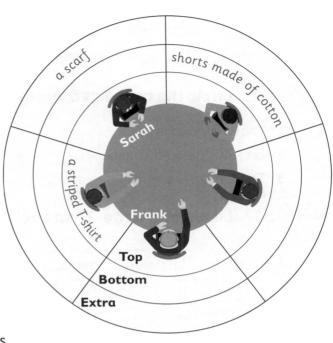

2 Draw a piece of clothing and write about it in your notebook.

These are my favourite long shorts. They're very, very big so I wear them with a belt. They're dark brown and they've got big pockets on the legs above the knees. My mum hates them, but I love them!

3 Describe the picture.

1 No one _____ is playing chess _____ .

2 Nothing _____ .
_____ .

3 No one _____ .
_____ .

4 Everyone _____ .
_____ .

5 Someone _____ .
_____ .

Sounds and life skills
Planning together
Pronunciation focus

1 🎧 **19** **Circle the connected words. Listen and check. Then say.**

1 That's a (good idea)!
2 Let's decide on the music.
3 That jacket is great!
4 Come on … hurry up.
5 Look at all the balloons.

2 🎧 **20** **Listen and write. Then circle the connected letters.**

1 Let's ___pla(n o)ur___ disco!   Can we _____ it _____ ?

2 We need to _____ on _____ day.   I think Friday _____ is best.

3 How _____ a big pizza?   I _____ Italian food!

4 Let's _____ up a _____ of balloons!   We've got _____ of ideas!

3 🎧 **21** **Listen and circle the correct information.**

1 **a** disco   (**b** party)   5 **a** green costumes   **b** silver costumes
2 **a** June   **b** September   6 **a** rock music   **b** electronic music
3 **a** 6.30   **b** 7.30   7 **a** star cakes   **b** moon cookies
4 **a** space   **b** aliens   8 **a** playground   **b** sports centre

4 **Complete with words from Activity 3.**

We're having a ___party___ on Friday 22nd
_____ at _____ in the evening.
The theme is _____ so please wear gold
or _____ .
There will be _____ _____ and _____ _____ !
It's going to be **OUT OF THIS WORLD** and out in the _____ !

1 Read and answer.

1 What did Aztec braves wear? _They wore birds' feathers and animal fur._
2 How did everyone feel when they saw them? _____
3 What did the Mayas do in the round building? _____
4 Why do they have to move fast? _____
5 When do the bowls work like mirrors? _____
6 At what time is the Sun at its highest? _____

2 Put the verbs into the past simple.

The Aztecs (1) ___were___ (are) very rich. They (2) _____ (have) fields and water to grow plants for food and materials. They also (3) _____ (have) lots of stone for building, and gold and silver. Like the Mayas, they (4) _____ (get) the liquid from rubber trees and (5) _____ (use) that too. They (6) _____ (make) balls for their famous ball game and (7) _____ (use) it to clean their teeth after meals. They (8) _____ (invent) the first chewing gum! Rich Aztec people (9) _____ (wear) more clothes than poor people, and their clothes (10) _____ (are) made from different cloth. Poor people (11) _____ (can't) wear cotton. Women and girls (12) _____ (make) most of their cloth from the 'century plant' and (13) _____ (use) bright colours and designs to decorate it. They (14) _____ (make) shoes from rubber, but if they (15) _____ (have) to go into a temple or see the king, they (16) _____ (can't) wear anything on their feet. When they (17) _____ (dance), they (18) _____ (wear) belts with sea shells to make music as they (19) _____ (move). They sometimes (20) _____ (wear) feathers and animal fur too. Aztec braves (21) _____ (paint) their faces to look horrible and to make people afraid of them. Married women (22) _____ (put) their hair up on top of their heads. Corn (23) _____ (is) their most important food, but they also (24) _____ (eat) a lot of vegetables. They (25) _____ (don't eat) a lot of meat, but they sometimes (26) _____ (eat) insects and lizards.

Do you remember?

1 It might ___rain___ later so I'm going to take an umbrella.
2 I need to study because we _____ have a maths test tomorrow, but I'm not sure.
3 I've got a new _____ so my trousers don't fall down.
4 When it's cold, I wear _____ on my hands.
5 People sewed _____ into their clothes 300 years ago.
6 _____ are usually made of nylon or wool.

Can do

I can talk about possibility using **may** and **might**.	☹	☺	😀
I can talk about clothes.	☹	☺	😀
I can write about my favourite clothes.	☹	☺	😀

What happens to our old trainers?

1 Read and write 'could' or 'if'.

Upcycling Tips
for Old Clothes

Do you ever think about how you can give your clothes a new life?
Read these tips for some great ideas!

1 You ___could___ turn some old T-shirts into a simple bag.

2 Have your socks got holes in them? You _____ turn them into sock monkey toys for a younger brother or sister!

3 _____ you can't get your old white trainers clean, make them more fashionable by adding glitter!

4 _____ your trousers are too old, cut them into shorts.

5 Do a clothes swap with some friends _____ you want a change.

6 Of course, you _____ take your old clothes to a second-hand shop.

2 Plan to write a leaflet. Complete the table about how to upcycle clothes.

Upcycling project:	
Information	Do you ever think about _____?
	Did you know that _____?
Advice	Here are some ideas to make your _____ last longer.
	You could _____.
	You could _____.
	If _____.
	If _____.

3 📝 Use your notes to write your leaflet.

4 Did you ...

☐ plan your leaflet?

☐ include some information and advice on your item of clothing?

☐ use **could** and **if** to give advice?

☐ check grammar, spelling and punctuation?

Writing tip

Writing a leaflet

A leaflet gives information and advice to help other people decide what to do. When you give advice, use **could** and **if**.

If you don't like your old clothes any more, you **could** give them to a friend instead.

Design: fashion and the environment | 🛡 social responsibility

Flyers Listening Part 4

1 🎧 22 **Listen and tick (✓) the box. There is one example.**

What has Holly put on to go to the park?

A   B ☐ C ☐

1 Where has Richard left his umbrella?

  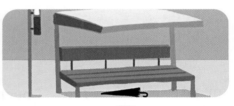

A ☐ B ☐ C ☐

2 Where is William going to go for his holiday?

A ☐ B ☐ C ☐

3 Which trousers will Emma wear to the party?

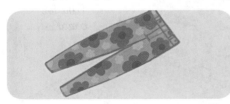  

A ☐ B ☐ C ☐

4 Where is Helen's brown belt now?

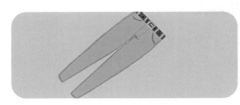  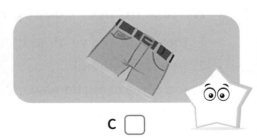

A ☐ B ☐ C ☐

8 Around the world

Have you finished **yet**?	I've **just** finished this book.
I haven't finished **yet**.	I've **already** finished my project.

1 Find two irregular past participles for each group of letters.

1 b- _been_ , _begun_
2 m- _____ , _____
3 dr- _____ , _____
4 t- _____ , _____
5 th- _____ , _____
6 br- _____ , _____

7 sp- _____ , _____
8 l- _____ , _____
9 c- _____ , _____
10 st- _____ , _____
11 r- _____ , _____
12 go- _____ , _____

aught   ome   ood   ought   rown   eant   ~~een~~   eft   ost   aken
un   olen   oken   aught   t   ought   ~~egun~~   et   iven   oken   ne   idden   awn

2 Complete the sentences with verbs from Activity 1.

1 He's r_idden_ his bike for two hours.
2 They've just g_____ out.
3 This is the third time I've b_____ to read this book!

4 She hasn't s_____ all her money yet.
5 Our cat still hasn't c_____ home.
6 They've just d_____ a picture.

3 Look and write sentences with 'already' 'yet' or 'just'.

1 (get up) _She's just got up._
2 (tidy her room) _She hasn't tidied her room yet._
3 (make her bed) _____
4 (put on her shoes) _____
5 (have breakfast) _____
6 (put on her trousers) _____

Come on! Time for breakfast!

4 Write sentences about you today. Use 'already', 'yet' or 'just'.

1 (have lunch) _I've already had lunch. / I haven't had lunch yet. / I've just had lunch._
2 (read something) _____
3 (do some of my homework) _____
4 (listen to music) _____

Language: present perfect with *just, yet, already*   Do the online activities on **Practice Extra** as you complete this unit

1 Tick (✓) two more correct sentences. Correct two more sentences.

1 'Tidy your room!' 'I've already tidied it!' ✓ _____
2 He is done his homework already. <u>He's already done his homework.</u>_____
3 Has he been to Australia? _____
4 I live here for ten years. _____
5 They's seen that film already. _____
6 She's studied English for three years. _____

2 What have they just done? Complete the sentences.

<u>He's just tidied his room</u> .

She _____ .

They _____ .

She _____ .

We _____ .

He _____ .

3 Look at the Hirds' plans. Read and answer 'Yes, they have.' or 'No, they haven't.'

Holiday!

		morning	afternoon
Monday	Cambridge	see the university	play in a park
Tuesday	Nottingham	see the castle	ride bikes in Sherwood Forest
Wednesday	Liverpool	cross the River Mersey	go shopping
Thursday	York	have a picnic near the Roman walls	go to the Viking Museum
Friday	London	visit the Science Museum	take a photo of Big Ben

Now it is Wednesday lunchtime.

1 The Hirds haven't seen Cambridge University yet. <u>Yes, they have.</u>_____
2 They've already ridden bikes in Sherwood Forest. _____
3 They've already crossed the River Mersey. _____
4 They haven't had a picnic near the Roman walls . _____
5 They've already taken a photo of Big Ben. _____
6 They haven't visited the Science Museum yet. _____

1 Label the car stickers with nationalities. Use the letters in the box.

(**E**)   (**GR**)

| ~~a~~ a a a a a c c d |
| e e e e e e g ~~h~~ |
| h ~~i~~ i i i k l m ~~n~~ |
| n n n n n n o ~~p~~ r |
| r r r r ~~s~~ s t u u x |
| z B F G G I M P ~~s~~ |

(**IND**)   (**D**)

1 _Spanish_   3 _____   5 _____   7 _____

(**BR**)   (**P**)

(**F**)   (**MEX**)

2 _____   4 _____   6 _____   8 _____

2 What countries are these web pages from?

www.mundocrianças.br	1 _Brazil_
www.xiaohaizi.cn	2 _____
www.niñolandia.es	3 _____
www.mondenfant.fr	4 _____

www.kidsofindia.in	5 _____
www.sunfun4kids.gr	6 _____
www.4crianças.pt	7 _____
www.mundoniños.mx	8 _____

3 Read and answer.

Did you know that there are 195 countries in the world? Each of them has a capital city. Some of them even have more than one capital and South Africa has three capitals! Some capitals aren't difficult to learn. For example, it's easy to remember that Mexico City is the capital of Mexico or that Brasilia is the capital of Brazil. We know the names of other capitals because we hear about them in lessons at school, the news or sporting events.

You might know that the capital of Spain is Madrid and the capital of Greece is Athens. You may even know that the Chinese capital is Beijing or that the Portuguese capital is Lisbon, but did you know that the Indian capital is New Delhi? Some capitals surprise us because they aren't the biggest city in the country. Did you know that the capital of Australia isn't Sydney? No, it's Canberra, and the capital of the USA isn't New York. It's Washington D.C.

1 What's the Mexican capital? _It's Mexico City._

2 What's the capital of India? _____

3 Which country is Canberra the capital of? _____

4 What's the name of the Chinese capital? _____

5 What's the Spanish capital? _____

6 What's the capital of Portugal? _____

7 Which country is Washington D.C. the capital of? _____

8 What's the Brazilian capital? _____

Vocabulary: countries and nationalities

Complete the words with the groups of letters in the box. Use each group for only one pair of words.

> al   any   ch   co   ey   ~~me~~   sh   tal   th   try

1 Ro...   ___me___   ...tal   Yes   (No)
2 Turk...   _____   ...es   Yes   No
3 coun...   _____   ...ing   Yes   No
4 Germ...   _____   ...where   Yes   No
5 Fren...   _____   ...opsticks   Yes   No

6 Portug...   _____   ...ready   Yes   No
7 capi...   _____   ...lest   Yes   No
8 Engli...   _____   ...orts   Yes   No
9 nor...   _____   ...rown   Yes   No
10 Mexi...   _____   ...mb   Yes   No

2 **Say the pairs of words in Activity 1. Do the letters sound the same in both words? Circle 'Yes' or 'No'.**

> Rome ... metal

3 **Ask and answer. Write your partner's answers.**

1 Have you ever eaten Spanish food?   _____   What was it? _____
2 Have you ever eaten Mexican food?   _____   What was it? _____
3 Have you ever eaten Indian food?   _____   What was it? _____
4 Have you ever eaten Portuguese food?   _____   What was it? _____
5 Have you ever eaten Italian food?   _____   What was it? _____
6 Have you ever eaten Chinese food?   _____   What was it? _____
7 Have you ever eaten _____ food?   What was it? _____
8 Have you ever eaten _____ food?   What was it? _____

4 **Write a report about international food that you and your partner have eaten.**

We haven't eaten Chinese food, but I've eaten Portuguese food. I can't remember the word,

but it was fish with tomatoes. It was delicious. Igor's eaten Mexican food.

_____

_____

_____

_____

_____

_____

_____

_____

_____

Sounds and life skills
Understanding responsibilities

Pronunciation focus

 1 🎧 23 **Listen and underline the stressed words.**

1 I've <u>already</u> <u>tidied</u> my <u>desk</u>.
2 Wait! I haven't saved the article yet!
3 Have they given the names of the competition winners yet?
4 We've just won new tablets for everyone in our class!

 2 **Complete. Then practise saying the sentences.**

1 I've already _____ .
2 Wait! I haven't _____ yet!
3 Have they _____ yet?
4 We've just _____ !

 3 **Read and match.**

1 bus driver   I've just seen an island.   I haven't sung in Rome or London.
2 chef   I've sung in New York and Paris.   I haven't explored it yet.
3 journalist   I've already designed the rocket.   I've just taken the children to school.
4 pirate   I've already made the salads.   I haven't written the story yet.
5 pop star   I've already taken photos.   I haven't built it yet.
6 engineer   I've already washed the bus.   I haven't made the apple pie yet.

 4 **Read and complete.**

Every day, I have to _____ .
Before I go to school, I have to _____ .
At school, I need to _____ and _____ .
After school, I have to _____ .

1 Read and answer.

Diggory Bones

1 What's Iyam just done? <u>He's just pushed the corn symbol.</u>
2 How long has the museum at Balankanche been open? _____
3 How did the Mayas water their fields? _____
4 How long have Interpol wanted Iyam and Richard Tricker? _____
5 What are Sir Doug Bones and Diggory going to do with the Sun Stone? _____
6 What did Emily's grandfather use to follow them? _____

2 Do the Mayan quiz. True (T) or False (F)?

1 The Aztecs built the modern day Mexico City on a lake called Texcoco because they saw a Quetzal bird there. **T /Ⓕ**
2 The Mayas studied the sun, the moon and the stars to measure time. **T / F**
3 For the Aztecs, gold was the most important material in their lives. **T / F**
4 The Mayas used picture writing or 'glyphs' to communicate by writing. **T / F**
5 The Mayas played musical instruments made of turtle shells, wood and sea shells. **T / F**
6 The Pyramid of Kukulcan sounds like a Quetzal bird singing when someone climbs it. **T / F**
7 The Mayas played a ball game called Tlachtli. It's like volleyball and basketball. **T / F**
8 Aztec braves painted their faces and wore birds' feathers and animal fur to look beautiful and to make people love them. **T / F**
9 The first chewing gum was made from soft rubber from trees. The Mayas used it to clean their teeth. **T / F**
10 The form of a snake moves up and down the north stairs of the Pyramid of The Sun. **T / F**

Do you remember?

1 It's seven o'clock in the evening. Have you done your homework ___yet___?
2 Yes, I've _____ finished it! I finished it ten seconds ago.
3 Paris is the _____ of France.
4 People in Mexico speak _____ .
5 I have been to Germany and France but I can't speak _____ or _____ .
6 Beijing is the capital of _____ .

Can do

I can talk about what has happened using **just, already** and **yet**.

I can talk about different countries and nationalities.

I can write about things I've done.

Which countries do people visit most?

 Read and match.

My holiday in Malaysia

1 The capital city of Malaysia is Kuala Lumpur, which is also the
2 In Kuala Lumpur you can visit the tallest
3 Malaysian food is amazing, and the most
4 I think the most beautiful
5 There is a lot of traffic, so for me, the

a park is KLCC Park in the city centre.
b biggest city.
c easiest way to travel around the city is by train.
d twin skyscrapers in the world – the Petronas Twin Towers.
e popular food is nasi lemak, which is rice cooked in coconut milk.

 Plan to write a blog post. Complete the table about a holiday.

Paragraph 1 Where did you go? When did you go? Who did you go with?	I went to _____ on holiday. I went on/in _____. I went with _____. We stayed _____.
Paragraph 2 Where is it? What else do you know? What is it famous for?	_____ is a town/city/country in _____. The official language is _____. The weather there is _____. It is famous for its _____.
Paragraph 3 What did you see/do/eat?	For me, the most interesting place was _____. The best thing I saw was _____.
Paragraph 4 How do you feel about your holiday?	It was _____. _____

 Use your notes to write your blog post.

 Did you ...
- ☐ plan your blog post?
- ☐ talk about what to see, do and eat?
- ☐ use superlatives?
- ☐ read your blog post again?
- ☐ check your grammar, spelling and punctuation?

Writing tip

Writing a blog post

We use superlatives to describe things. You can use superlatives in a blog post to give more information and describe how you felt.

The **best** thing to do there is ...
The **hottest** season is ...

Maths: graphs and charts | learning to learn

Flyers Reading and Writing Part 6

1 **Read the diary and write the missing words. Write one word on each line.**

Example   This evening I'm writing my diary ___in___ Paris!

1   Paris is the capital of _____ . I'm here because I want to learn

2   to _____ French better and to see the city, of course. Today I

3   _____ to the Eiffel Tower with my friends. It's really tall and it

4   looks very beautiful. I _____ some great photos.

5   Tomorrow we're _____ to visit a famous museum which is

         called the Louvre, so we can see the 'Mona Lisa'. I can't wait!

Review Units 7 and 8

1 **Read the story. Choose a word from the box. Write the correct word next to numbers 1–8.**

> belt   button   capital   clothes   different   ~~just~~   Paris   pockets
> same   shorts   Spanish   T-shirt   trousers   umbrellas   worn

FRIENDLY

Stella, Meera and Lenny are sad because the second series of **Friendly** has _____ just _____ ended. They all agree that the funniest episode of this series was 'Jim's new clothes'.

In this episode Jim and Peter went to London to buy some new clothes. They caught the train to the (1) _____ one Saturday morning. They found a shop called Fine Fashion. The salesman told them that all the clothes came from (2) _____ , the capital of France and the capital of fashion.

Jim bought some big, green trousers with (3) _____ above the knees. He bought a light-grey T-shirt and a black (4) _____ . He liked his new (5) _____ and he decided to wear them home.

When they went back to the station, they saw Jim's grandfather, but it was very funny because his grandpa's (6) _____ were big and green with pockets above the knees. He was also wearing a light-grey (7) _____ and a black belt. His clothes were the (8) _____ as Jim's!

2 **Now choose the best name for the story.**

Tick one box.   Streets ahead ☐   Capital cities ☐   The latest fashion ☐

3 **Read and match the jokes.**

1 What do you call an elephant at the North Pole?
2 What did the scarf say to the hat?
3 Why do birds fly south in winter?
4 What must we break before we can use it?
5 What kind of key opens a banana?
6 What do you get if you cross a kangaroo with an elephant?
7 What do you call an elephant with a carrot in each ear?
8 What do sea monsters eat?
9 How far can you walk into the wood?
10 What's the best thing to put into ice cream?

a   Anything! It can't hear you!   ☐
b   A monkey!   ☐
c   A spoon!   ☐
d   Lost!   ☐ 1
e   Because it's easier than walking!   ☐
f   Half way. Then you're walking out of the wood.   ☐
g   You go on ahead, I'll just hang around.   ☐
h   Big holes in Australia!   ☐
i   An egg!   ☐
j   Fish and ships.   ☐

4 Complete the sentences. Count and write the letters.

1 _____Shorts_____ are short trousers. We wear them in summer. [6]

2 Hindi, French and Portuguese are different _____ . [ ]

3 We wear _____ on our hands. [ ]

4 A hundred years is a _____ [ ]

5 He's just _____ his coat on. He's going out. [ ]

6 Africa is a _____ . [ ]

7 You might have a _____ inside your jacket. You can carry things in it. [ ]

8 The cities of London, Paris and Rome are all _____ . [ ]

9 We use this to close our shirts and coats. It can be different shapes and colours. _____ [ ]

10 We wear a _____ at the top of our trousers or jeans so they don't fall down. [ ]

11 China is a _____ . [ ]

12 Oh, no! It's just started to rain and I've left my _____ at home! [ ]

13 We wear _____ on our feet, often to do sport. [ ]

14 Special clothes to protect us. A fire fighter wears one. _____ [ ]

5 Now complete the crossword. Write the message.

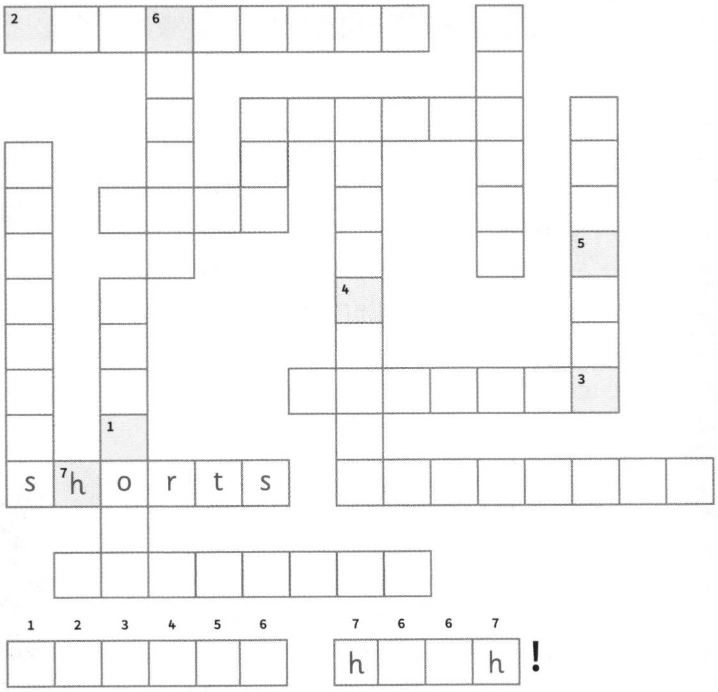

(crossword grid)

s | 7h | o | r | t | s

| 1 | 2 | 3 | 4 | 5 | 6 | | 7 | 6 | 6 | 7 |
| | | | | | | | h | | | h | !

6 Quiz time!

1 Why was Lenny's shirt funny at the disco?
It was _____

2 When did people start wearing trainers? _____

3 How long does plastic take to decompose? _____

4 How many countries won the blog competition? _____

5 Where is sushi from? _____

6 What was the most popular country for people to visit in 2019? _____

7 Write questions for your quiz in your notebook.

Living with technology

1 **Read and answer.**

David's older sister, Jenny, thinks he's got a problem with computers. He spends more than two hours a day in front of the screen and he's very unhappy when he hasn't got an internet connection. He spends all weekend at home playing on the computer and he doesn't want to go out with his friends.

When his parents call him for family meals he takes about ten minutes to go to the table. Then he gets angry when he has to help the family to clean up after the meal. He only wants to go back to the computer. Last Sunday, Jenny saw him playing games on the computer at three o'clock in the morning when the family were all in bed.

1 Who thinks David's got a problem? _Jenny thinks he's got a problem._
2 How much time does he spend on the computer every day? _____
3 Why doesn't he want to go out with his friends? _____
4 What was he doing at three o'clock in the morning last Sunday? _____
5 Do you think David's got a problem? _____
6 What do you think Jenny should do? _____
_____

2 **Write sentences with 'should' or 'shouldn't'.**

1 be careful / talk to / internet _You should be careful who you talk to on the internet._
2 spend time / in front of / screen _____
3 be afraid / use technology _____
4 play games / at night _____
5 get angry / use technology _____

Values: units 1 and 2 | social responsibility

Units 3&4 Values Being safe at home

1 **Read and choose the answer.**

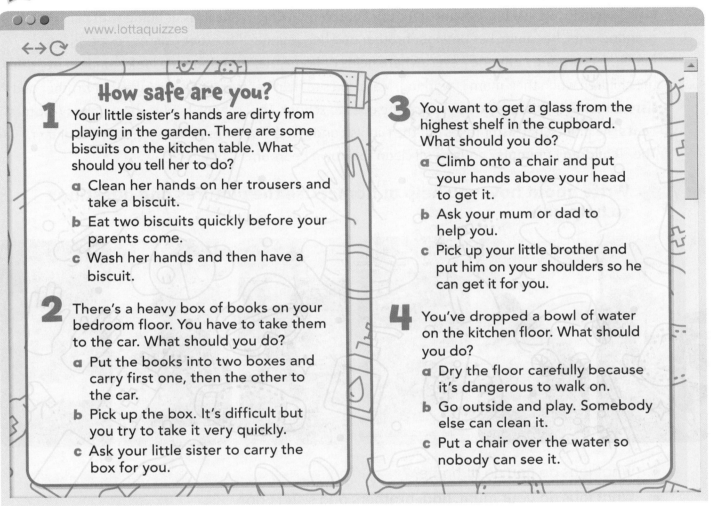

www.lottaquizzes

How safe are you?

1 Your little sister's hands are dirty from playing in the garden. There are some biscuits on the kitchen table. What should you tell her to do?

a Clean her hands on her trousers and take a biscuit.

b Eat two biscuits quickly before your parents come.

c Wash her hands and then have a biscuit.

2 There's a heavy box of books on your bedroom floor. You have to take them to the car. What should you do?

a Put the books into two boxes and carry first one, then the other to the car.

b Pick up the box. It's difficult but you try to take it very quickly.

c Ask your little sister to carry the box for you.

3 You want to get a glass from the highest shelf in the cupboard. What should you do?

a Climb onto a chair and put your hands above your head to get it.

b Ask your mum or dad to help you.

c Pick up your little brother and put him on your shoulders so he can get it for you.

4 You've dropped a bowl of water on the kitchen floor. What should you do?

a Dry the floor carefully because it's dangerous to walk on.

b Go outside and play. Somebody else can clean it.

c Put a chair over the water so nobody can see it.

2 **Write a safety contract for your home.**

1 We must put our toys away safely.
2 _____
3 _____
4 _____
5 _____

_____ got the Safety at Home certificate.

✓ **Congratulations!**

Units 5&6 Values Helping at home

1 **Read and choose the right words.**

Mei Li's family live in a big [1] **country** / **city** / **continent** in China. She lives at home with her grandparents, her mum, her younger brother and her younger [2] **brother** / **sister** / **aunt**. In her family, [3] **everyone** / **anyone** / **everywhere** helps at home. Her grandparents look [4] **under** / **at** / **after** the children when their mum is working. Mei Li likes to help her family, so she takes her brother and sister to school, [5] **before** / **after** / **since** she goes to school. After school, her brother [6] **feeds** / **waters** / **eats** the plants, her sister takes out the rubbish and Mei Li [7] **washes** / **cooks** / **cleans** the dinner. The [8] **children** / **animals** / **cousins** all clean their own bedrooms.

2 **Write about how you help at home. Use the pictures and questions to help you.**

- What jobs do you do at home?
- What jobs do your mum, dad, brothers and sisters do?
- Do you enjoy doing jobs at home? Why? Why not?
- How do you feel when you help at home?

At home, I do several things to help.

Values: units 5 and 6 | social responsibility

Units 7&8 Values Sharing problems

1 Read and answer.

1 There's a new boy at school. How can you help him to make friends?

2 Some children at school have started calling you horrible names. What should you do?

3 Your little brother has a big problem at school. He's asked you not to tell anybody.
You think the problem is serious. What are you going to do?

4 Your group of friends at school don't like another student. They've told you not to spend time
with this student or they won't talk to you. What should you do?

5 One of your friends has sent some horrible messages to another student at school. What are
you going to do?

2 Talk about your ideas with your partner. Do you agree?

> I agree.

> I don't agree. I think …

3 Read and match.

1	I'm very	a	I do?	
2	They think	b	angry.	1
3	This isn't	c	very worried.	
4	What should	d	help me.	
5	I feel	e	the first time.	
6	Please	f	it's funny.	

4 Write a message to a friend about a problem you have at school in your notebook. Use phrases from Activity 3 to help you.

5 Swap your message with a partner. Read the message and then give them some advice.

> You should / shouldn't …

> You have to …

> The best idea is to …

> You must / mustn't …

Grammar reference

⭐ **Complete the sentences.** [don't Let's mustn't Shall should ~~Would~~]

1 _____Would_____ you like an ice cream?
2 You _____ play football in the road.
3 Why _____ we send her a text message?
4 _____ we chat online?
5 I _____ do my homework before I play on the computer.
6 _____ write an article for the blog.

1 **Write questions. Answer.**

1 he / be an actor? (✗) Is he going to be an actor?   No, he isn't.
2 they / see a film? (✓) _____   _____
3 you / do your homework? (✓) _____   _____
4 she / be in the play? (✗) _____   _____
5 we / play tennis? (✗) _____   _____
6 he / read a book about dragons? (✓) _____   _____

2 **Read and write.**

1 They'll go to the moon by plane. (rocket) No, they won't. They'll go there by rocket.
2 She'll eat fruit. (special food) _____
3 I'll wear jeans. (skirt) _____
4 They'll fly to Jupiter. (Mars) _____
5 We'll leave next week. (next month) _____
6 There'll be a lot of people. (robots) _____

3 **Read and match.**

1 I was snowboarding
2 They were waiting at the bus
3 She was making bread
4 We were having a picnic when
5 I was walking through the
6 He was sleeping when he

a felt a mouse in his sleeping bag.
b forest when I dropped my torch.
c when she lost her ring.
d when I fell and hurt my elbow.
e the storm began.
f stop when they saw their friend.

☐ ☐ ☐ [1] ☐ ☐

4 **Read and circle the correct word.**

1 There are too (many)/ any knives.
2 There isn't / aren't enough chairs.
3 She hasn't got much / many sugar.
4 They haven't got too / enough forks.
5 Did they have much / many sweets?
6 How many / much pasta do you want?

5 **Complete the sentences. Write 'for' or 'since'.**

1 She's had her computer _____ since _____ 2020.

2 We've studied English _____ five years.

3 I haven't played tennis _____ two weeks.

4 They've lived here _____ they were six.

5 He's been at his new school _____ three months.

6 She hasn't seen Peter _____ the summer.

6 **Complete the sentences.**

> any   anything   ~~Everything~~   no one   something   somewhere

1 It's raining. _____ Everything _____ in the garden is wet.

2 I saw _____ interesting on TV last night.

3 The house was empty because _____ was at home.

4 He didn't have _____ money so he didn't go to the cinema.

5 I want to go _____ exciting on holiday this year.

6 Our town is really boring for young people. There isn't _____ to do.

7 **Read and order the words.**

1 (go to) (this evening.) (We might) (the cinema)

We might go to the cinema this evening.

2 (I'm tired.) (leave the disco) (I may) (early because)

_____

3 (They may not) (their project.) (have time) (to finish)

_____

4 (because of the snow.) (let us go home) (The teacher might) (early today)

_____

8 **Write the sentences in the present perfect. Use the words given.**

1 (just) I arrive at the airport. I've just arrived at the airport.

2 (yet) He not be to New York. _____

3 (already) I tidy my room. _____

4 (yet) you write that email? _____

5 (just) He wake up. _____

6 (already) They finish the book. _____

Irregular verbs

Infinitive	Past tense	Past participle
be	was / were	been
be called	was / were called	been called
be going to	was / were going to	been going to
begin	began	begun
break	broke	broken
bring	brought	brought
buy	bought	bought
can	could	–
catch	caught	caught
choose	chose	chosen
come	came	come
cut	cut	cut
do	did	done
draw	drew	drawn
drink	drank	drunk
drive	drove	driven
dry	dried	dried
eat	ate	eaten
fall	fell	fallen
fall over	fell over	fallen over
feel	felt	felt
find	found	found
find out	found out	found out
fly	flew	flown
forget	forgot	forgotten
get	got	got
get (un)dressed	got (un)dressed	got (un)dressed
get (up / on / off)	got (up / on / off)	got (up / on / off)
get to	got to	got to
give	gave	given
go	went	gone / been
go out	went out	gone / been out
go shopping	went shopping	gone / been shopping
grow	grew	grown
have	had	had
have got	had	had
have (got) to	had to	had to
hear	heard	heard
hide	hid	hidden
hit	hit	hit
hold	held	held
hurt	hurt	hurt
keep	kept	kept
know	knew	known

Infinitive	Past tense	Past participle
learn	learnt / learned	learnt / learned
leave	left	left
let	let	let
lie down	lay down	lain down
lose	lost	lost
make	made	made
make sure	made sure	made sure
mean	meant	meant
meet	met	met
must	had to	had to
put	put	put
put on	put on	put on
read	read	read
ride	rode	ridden
run	ran	run
say	said	said
see	saw	seen
sell	sold	sold
send	sent	sent
should	–	–
sing	sang	sung
sit	sat	sat
sleep	slept	slept
smell	smelt / smelled	smelt / smelled
speak	spoke	spoken
spell	spelt / spelled	spelt / spelled
spend	spent	spent
stand	stood	stood
steal	stole	stolen
swim	swam	swum
swing	swung	swung
take	took	taken
take a photo / picture	took a photo / picture	taken a photo / picture
take off	took off	taken off
teach	taught	taught
tell	told	told
think	thought	thought
throw	threw	thrown
understand	understood	understood
wake up	woke up	woken up
wear	wore	worn
win	won	won
write	wrote	written